"If you want to better unders[...] prophecy, then read this bo[...] journalist, Ralph Stice is a [...] approach to his analysis of why the Arab Spring had to happen and what Western Christians can do to prepare for the future. This book will help ensure that your faith is built on Christ alone and the assurance of spending eternity with Him, not the sometimes-scary flow of history. You will also get a complete education on Islam and its possible role in the End Times."

Joel Richardson
New York Times bestselling author
and internationally recognized teacher

"As followers of Jesus Christ, in a world quickly changing and contorting around us, it is urgent that we understand what is happening in terms of religion, politics, and the implications for our faith. It is the appropriate time for *Arab Spring, Christian Winter*. Information and entertainment continue to blend together with facts, propaganda, and appeasing words, forming our headlines and storylines. What are we to believe and from whose perspective is the story being told? What are the implications to the Church and to us as Christ-followers? Ralph takes us through a fact-based look at Islam and Islamism in the present day and in a way the world can understand. We must be informed and prepared. We must pray without ceasing. For those whose house is built upon the Rock, the water is rising..."

Edward Anderson
Global Chief Information Officer, World Vision International

"What a book! I have heard Ralph lecture on the teachings and practice of Islam with great interest and intrigue. Personally, I consider Ralph Stice to be one of the most trustworthy and exceptionally well-qualified commentators on this subject. Having read his book I can assure you it is one of the most riveting and informative readings you will find on the subject of Islam. For me it is a must-read for every Christian who is searching for answers and information on the present rise and expansion of this sometimes-dangerous religion."

Dr. Allan Bosson
Senior Pastor of Southside Baptist Church, Savannah, Georgia

"*Arab Spring, Christian Winter* is a wake-up call for the American Church and is a MUST-READ for anyone who considers themselves a Christian. Ralph has spent years living among Muslims in three nations and has spent countless hours in deep discussion of their faith. In this book, the reader gains rare prophetic insight into their point of view and the risks they pose to American Christians."

Jeffrey D. Voudrie
President, Common Sense Advisors

ARAB SPRING
CHRISTIAN WINTER

About the cover: *the Arabic letter pictured in red is pronounced "noon" and is the letter "N" in that language. It is the first letter of the word "nasara," which means "Nazarene," or Christian. It was recently spray-painted in red on the homes of Christians in Mosul, Iraq, by Islamic State (ISIS) soldiers to denote families that would have to make a choice: convert to Islam, pay an exorbitant tax, leave the area, or die. Christians around the world have posted this letter in social media and worn it on T-shirts to signify their solidarity with persecuted Christian brothers and sisters in ISIS-controlled lands. It has become a one-letter symbol of Christian genocide in the Middle East.*

ARAB SPRING
CHRISTIAN WINTER

Islam Unleashed on the Church and the World

Ralph Stice

ANEKO Press

Visit Ralph's website: www.rwsministries.com:

Arab Spring, Christian Winter – Ralph Stice

Copyright © 2014

First edition published 2014

Scriptures taken from the Holy Bible, New International Version®, NIV®. Copyright © 1973, 1978, 1984, 2011 by Biblica, Inc.™ Used by permission of Zondervan. All rights reserved worldwide www.zondervan.com. The "NIV" and "New International Version" are trademarks registered in the United States Patent and Trademark Office by Biblica, Inc.™

Author Photo: Dylan Wilson

Cover Design: Amber Burger

Editors: Nancy L. Graves, Ruth Zetek

Printed in the United States of America

www.lifesentencepublishing.com

LIFE SENTENCE Publishing books are available at discounted prices for ministries and other outreach.

Find out more by contacting us at info@lspbooks.com

ANEKO Press, LIFE SENTENCE Publishing, and its logo are trademarks of LIFE SENTENCE Publishing, LLC

P.O. Box 652

Abbotsford, WI 54405

RELIGION / Biblical Studies / Prophecy

Paperback ISBN: 978-1-62245-233-0

Ebook ISBN: 978-1-62245-234-7

10 9 8 7 6 5 4 3 2 1

This book is available from www.amazon.com, Barnes & Noble, and your local bookstore.

Share this book on Facebook:

Contents

Introduction

The young man has the start of a healthy beard. Dark, wavy hair. Bushy eyebrows. He dressed himself in several layers before going out that August morning in Mosul, Iraq.

He could be my son.

It's his eyes that haunt me. They opened briefly as he perhaps realized what had just happened to him, that soldiers from the Islamic State of Iraq and Syria (ISIS) had cut his throat, and now he lay on the ground woozy and wounded.

As I watched one of the many "contains disturbing images" videos showing the brutality of ISIS forces in Iraq and Syria, those eyes had a message for me: "Tell the world." They burned in my mind as I finished this book, reminding me of a line from my first book, *From 9/11 to 666,* when my family watched the live feed from New York on September 11 in our apartment outside of Paris, and I blurted: "We should have warned them."[1]

Now, as many Westerners discover the ancient way that a conquering Islamic army advances, courtesy of YouTube videos and Google images, that line echoes louder.

After reading this book, consider yourself warned.

This is what Muslims practice, and have practiced since the inception of Islam. Throughout history they have beheaded infidels who resist the onslaught of Islamic forces. As I write, it is "back to the future" in Iraq and Syria, a return to the

---

1   Ralph W. Stice, *From 9/11 to 666: The Convergence of Current Events, Biblical Prophecy and the Vision of Islam* (Ozark, AL: ACW Press, 2005), 23.

Golden Age of Islam, circa AD 610 – precisely what millions of Muslims want.

People have written about religious conflict in the Middle East for centuries, and anyone alive today has grown up reading headlines about Israel defending itself against rocket attacks, revolutions and regime change in Iraq, and rumblings in many other nations from Saudi Arabia to Morocco.

Yet something feels different today. The troubles have become more personal for those of us who are Christians. We are learning every day about churches being desecrated, crosses being broken, families being driven out of their homes, and worst of all, brothers and sisters in Jesus being executed for their faith.

Despite meager media reporting of these killings, nearly all of us who follow Jesus have seen Facebook postings and blog articles about a Christian mother facing a death sentence in Sudan, an innocent Christian teen on trial for blasphemy in Pakistan, or an entire Christian village emptied in Syria or Iraq with hundreds dead. All of those biblical texts about persecution and running to the hills and not looking back seem a little closer when we see them fulfilled on the evening news.

Christians *are* running and *are* being handed over for persecution unto death, and Christians seem to be hated by just about all ethnic groups in the lands of the Bible.

Why has this fierce persecution broken out now? What makes this era of danger for Christians different from others?

The thesis of this book asserts that the most vicious side of Islam, what I will call Islamism, was loosed, once and for all, with the start of the Arab Spring in late 2010 – with no turning back the tide on this change in world events.

I maintain that the Arab Spring has become a true Christian Winter for believers in the countries impacted by the sweeping political changes in the Middle East, and the spread of Islamism will not reverse course. In fact, I think it will be *given power to wage war against God's holy people and to conquer them. And*

... given authority over every tribe, people, language and nation (Revelation 13:7), led by an Antichrist figure who will rule the world just before the return of Christ.

When Mohamed Bouazizi set himself on fire on December 17, 2010, in Sidi Bouzid, Tunisia, he had no idea that he was playing a part in the fulfillment of biblical prophecy. "Basboosa," as he was known in his town, knocked down the first domino in the rapid re-alignment of governments across the Middle East with his suicidal protest. Bouazizi – this catalyst for the Arab Spring – who has since won international awards posthumously, and has streets and squares named for him around the world, sparked the massive and ongoing reconfiguration of the political map in the Islamic world, allowing the voice of the people to be heard from Mauritania to Oman. This voice is *decidedly fundamentalist*, and needed to rise to the fore if Muslim nations were to veer closer to the prophet Muhammad's original vision for Islam and become a competing force in the world once again.

Nine years ago, in *From 9/11 to 666,* I laid out a case for Islam playing a key role in the End Times, knowing that Muslim nations needed to push out their secular governments to prepare for alignment under the messiah that Muslims await: al-Mahdi.

That's how Mohamed Bouazizi played a role in the fulfillment of biblical prophecy. Through his seemingly personal protest, he unwittingly unleashed a tide of Islamism that has not stopped spreading into governments around the world. The next step is for all of these Islamists to unite and pledge to fulfill the prophet Muhammad's original vision: a world entirely submitted to Allah (Sura 8:39).

I tried to describe in my first book what I saw coming in the Islamic world by detailing a major desire of Muslims in chapter 7, "The Replacement of Ruling Elites." I wasn't sure how it would happen, but God has begun the transformation. All is on track for a continued progression toward the rule of an Islamic Antichrist who will lead a powerful Islamic bloc of countries into a direct showdown with the West.

Suffice it to say that *nothing* that has occurred over the past nine years works against the realization of the thesis I offered in my book. I again humbly state that I could be completely wrong in my theory, but I pray that you will consider my points and, more importantly, build the type of faith you need to withstand trouble ahead – in whatever form it comes. We could absolutely live on planet Earth another two thousand years, but I believe many signs point to Christ's return within the next few decades. Among them are the outstanding progress made in the fulfillment of the Great Commission, which Jesus Himself used as the exemplar for the Last Days (Matthew 24:13), and the growing influence of Islam around the world, particularly strict fundamentalism.

Let me define "Islamism" from the outset as the interpretation of Islam that seamlessly blends religion into politics by holding two sacred tenets: 1) the Koran is the basis for any government and law, and 2) Islam is meant for the entire world.

This interpretation of Islam I do not see as "radical" or unusual. I call Islamism "pure Islam" because it most accurately captures the ideals of Muhammad and applies them to today.

With the continued repercussions of the Arab Spring still rocking the Muslim world, I feel it is time for a new book for the following reasons: 1) to examine how this massive movement fits into biblical prophecy; 2) to consider what it means for Christians around the world, specifically, the impact on Western Christ-followers; and 3) what should be done in anticipation of a growing fundamentalist Islamic bloc in the twenty-first century.

The Growth Market for Islamic Antichrist Books

Since the publishing of my book in 2005, it has been interesting to see how many other Christian authors have jumped onto the

Islamic Antichrist train. I do not follow the popular Christian personalities' scene very closely because I have lived overseas for much of my adult life. I have a few favorite Christian authors that I read again and again, so I am not always aware of the latest releases, but I do see intriguing titles when I walk through the Walmart book section or get emails from Christian Book Distributors. I am not suggesting that these authors got the idea of an Islamic Antichrist from me, but I also do not think this now-popular theory is a coincidence. Looking at the latest predictions of David Jeremiah, Hal Lindsey, Joel Rosenberg, and others, I would call them a second wave of authors who are predicting a very Islamic feel to the Last Days.

Two other authors published this idea about the same time I did. One, Joel Richardson, has gone on to achieve a measure of notoriety in having many fantastic insights into the role of Islam in the Last Days. He has built a solid ministry, publishing often and well, as he alerts the Christian community to the goals and prophecy of Islam. The other author, Robert Livingston, also published in advance of these latest titles, writing an excellent book, *Christianity and Islam: The Final Clash*, which was another great resource as I compiled my first book.

In recent years, I have not been very active on the publishing front. I spent two years in one of the key countries of the Middle East as a teacher in order to stay in touch with Islam's movements in the world. During that time, I had a contract on a book about exploring ministry to Muslims based on my first decade abroad, but this book was never printed due to the publisher's board fearing "Muslim backlash" in countries where it sold books. Now I am in the U.S. due to family health concerns, and again have time to dig into this important topic.

So why should you pay attention to my viewpoint? Because I believe I bring a unique mix of experience and expertise to the topic. I have lived on four continents, spending significant time living within the Islamic community, and therefore speak three languages fluently and am conversational in a fourth. I have spent countless hours reading about the topic and conversing with Muslim teachers and imams. Also, before beginning my missionary ministry, I had a journalistic background as a newspaper editor.

Additionally, I profess a deep love for the Muslim people. I would hope this would shield me from the charge of being a bigot and racist, but unfortunately, I know it does not in our politically correct age. People have sprayed graffiti on church signs where I am to speak, with the words "Hate Speech" a favorite tag. I won't spend time discussing what true hate speech is, but will say that no speech flowing out of a heart full of God's love for Muslims can be true hate speech. It all depends on your interpretation of what I have to say.

I can understand why moderate Muslims in the West may view this book as a work of hate speech, because I use the potentially explosive term "Antichrist" in conjunction with Islam and believe that pure Islam insists on world domination.

If enough Westerners read this perspective, they could make life on the street very uncomfortable for veiled Muslim women in their communities. I get that, but I also know I need to inform the Western public about where Islam intends to go, what Muslims anticipate in their own prophecies, and how this appears to dovetail perfectly with Scripture's description of a world leader who *will honor a god of fortresses* (Daniel 11:38) and be *given power to wage war against God's holy people* (Revelation 13:7). In short, I'm sorry that the truth hurts, as I reveal the factual goals of pure Islam and disseminate information about the final "Caliph" (successor to Muhammad), who sounds an awful lot like the biblical Antichrist.

The irony is that if I sat down with a moderate Muslim infuriated by my "hate speech," we would probably enjoy each other's company. He or she would understand that my words flow from a heart of love for Muslims, but also a love for truth.

I understand the moderate Muslims' desire to practice their faith in a quiet way and not feel the sting of discrimination in the West, but I would blame the tenets of pure Islam for how uncomfortable my Muslim friends feel. In other words, don't shoot the messenger.

I know for a fact that some of my Muslim friends around the world will read this book, or the comments about it, and our friendship will be ruined. While I am saddened by this, I also think someone has to speak plainly about what is happening in our world, and where phenomena like the Arab Spring can lead. While my moderate Muslim friends in the U.S., France, Côte d'Ivoire, and Turkey express their disappointment in me, they know that Muslims all over the globe do want *sharia* (Islamic law) applied in every country and long for one leader to direct them to global conquest. To my moderate friends I say, "The crazy uncle you have locked in the basement – Ishak Islamist we can call him – is now on his way to becoming king. You and I both regret that."

If moderate westernized Muslims could spend a little time with their brothers and sisters in Mosul, Tripoli, or Tunis, they would see Islam's more aggressive, conservative face gaining strength every day. I often think such cross-cultural exposure would be wonderful; it would help the moderate, educated Muslims possessing analytical abilities discover the heartbeat of their faith and, possibly, turn to the Prince of Peace as a desirable alternative. That was the message I drilled into brilliant high school students during my Critical Thinking course in Turkey. I taught, "If you don't like the fundamentalist Islamic version of God, there are other options out there for you to investigate. I know that anyone who seeks the Lord will find Him (see Deuteronomy 4:29)."

So, in response to widespread requests from readers of my first book to write an updated edition in light of the Arab Spring, I offer you this tome. It will not contain another timeline, which

I foolishly inserted in my first book because I believed God was in as big a hurry as I was. I have since been reminded in many ways that He is *never* in a hurry, and Jesus may not return in 2017! I will build my case further for an Islamic Antichrist based on the spectacular events that have transpired since 2005. Those eyes will allow me to do nothing less.

The World Now Is Much Better Prepared to Receive an Islamic Messiah

Again, this is where Basboosa comes in. He took a stand against a corrupt government and symbolized the frustrations of millions of Muslims who languished in similar countries ruled by corrupt despots. His suicide touched the heartstrings of Muslims around the world, and in less than eighteen months' time, the political map of the Middle East had radically changed. All of this was not an accident, as unlikely as it seemed in late 2010. At that point, it appeared that dictators from Tunisia to Libya to Egypt to Yemen would stay in power indefinitely. Then, traditionally, when they passed away, their sons would inherit their thrones and billion-dollar fortunes.

But God had other plans. In order for the Islamic bloc to be united in a vision for world domination, secular dictators would have to be swept aside. So that is what happened and continues to happen as I write.

If an Antichrist figure is to arise out of the Muslim world, then that world must be unified in the idea that Islam is the answer to all of humanity's problems. This brand of pure Islam requires the Koran to serve as a constitution and *sharia* law to govern society. It further believes that Islam is on a path to inevitable world domination where only two "houses" exist: Dar al-Harb and Dar al-Salaam – the house of war and the house of peace, with peace reigning where pure Islam resides. In the nations that resist this unstoppable tide, war must be waged until all peoples submit to Allah. We know as Christians that

God places rulers in power to accomplish His purposes, as difficult as that might seem for us.

> The Bible says, *He changes times and seasons; he deposes kings and raises up others. He gives wisdom to the wise and knowledge to the discerning* (Daniel 2:21), and *Let everyone be subject to the governing authorities, for there is no authority except that which God has established. The authorities that exist have been established by God* (Romans 13:1).

These verses and others like them are great reminders of God's sovereignty in history. They are needed today, as many Americans are sure that God's will was not done in the 2012 presidential election, and that God has become weak as governments who do not want to play nice with America multiply. These are the kind of bedrock verses to meditate on when a new government arises headed by an Islamic man seeming to be big trouble for Christ-followers. That day is coming. I hope to explain a bit more about how and why in this book.

You must drill down into the Rock and cling to Him as world events continue to mold the future.

Your faith cannot be shaken by whoever is in the driver's seat of any given government, American or Saudi Arabian. You must drill down into the Rock and cling to Him as world events continue to mold the future at a faster rate than ever seen before. That will be a large part of this book's message as well.

If an Islamic Antichrist is to arise, he must have a coalition of governments who are on the same page with him. Islamism must burn in the hearts not only of peasants in small villages or imams in rural mosques, but in the halls of power.

Today, in 2014, this is far truer than in 2005, a development that I predicted in my first book, as Muslims achieved the freedoms that most American foreign policymakers so desperately wanted for them in this past decade. As I said then, I say again: Be careful what you wish for.

Watch for constant action in Saudi Arabia, Turkey, Algeria, Tunisia, Syria and Pakistan. Leaders will be the targets of assassination, and as small victories pile up, the moderate middle will swing to the side they believe will emerge victorious. I believe the entire Islamic landscape will change in the next 10 years, setting the stage for events I will describe in the next chapter.[2]

Why Muslims Are So Excited These Days

There are still a few governments on that list that have yet to get in line with the prophet Muhammad's visualization of a world completely prepared for Allah's judgment, with Islam ruling from sea to shining sea. That scene has been well described by numerous Islamic authors and speakers who see the same developments as I do. Here is how they convey what is coming:

The End Times is a period close to the Day of Judgment when the morality of the Qur'an will prevail all over the world and will be prevalently lived by people all over the world. The immorality, persecution, violence, injustice and degeneration of the past times will disappear in this blessed period, all sorts of suffering will be replaced by abundance, wealth, beauty, peace and ease. There will be great developments in technology and all these will be put into use for the benefit of all people.[3]

This kind of talk is all over the Internet and on the pages of many books written in recent years by Islamic thinkers. They, and Christians, are witnessing the same events from completely different perspectives, which should not surprise anyone who knows about the turbulent history of the East and West through the centuries. The chief takeaway for you, the reader, is that Muslims believe:

---

2   Ibid., 153.

3   *http://harunyahya.com/en/51/categories/Mahdi-Jesus-and-the-End-Times* (a site of a prominent Turkish imam/author) (June 27, 2013).

- They will rule the world one day, no question about it.

- The world will come closest to perfection when Islam reigns.

- Once this rule is inaugurated, then Allah can rightly judge the world's people. He will do so soon after the Islamic messiah comes.

I trust that you can again see the fascinating parallels between Islamic thought and Christian thought. However, there are also massive differences. We Christians believe that we must prepare the world for judgment by spreading the gospel in peaceful ways, using all means necessary. The gospel always allows refusal, and those who decline God's offer of salvation in Christ are left to answer to the Lord Himself.

In Islam, by contrast, the world must be prepared through Islamic conquest of all nations through military or political means. The invitation to submit to Allah through Islam allows refusal, but the consequences of that rebuff are usually quick and tangible: a beheading, an oppressive tax on infidels, the prohibition of infidel houses of worship to be built, or second-class status as a *dhimmi*, or non-Muslim resident of an Islamic state. Many books have been written about the historical treatment of minority communities under Islam.[4] I have seen it with my own eyes, and trust me – it is not tolerant or pretty.

You might think, "That was centuries ago. It's not like that now. Muslims have learned to be tolerant like everyone else." I will give proof in this book that such is not the case in 2014, and would remind you that you have probably not had the experience of living in an Islamic country. If you have, you will not argue my point; if you haven't, you will see soon enough how pure Islam treats the infidels in its midst. For a couple

---

4   Bat Ye'or's books are a great primer in this genre of literature. I would rec-
    ommend *The Dhimmi: Jews and Christians Under Islam* and *The Decline
    of Eastern Christianity under Islam: From Jihad to Dhimmitude: Seventh-
    Twentieth Century*.

quick examples to give you pause, tell me what you can do with a Christian corpse in Saudi Arabia, or how Egypt's Coptic Christians are faring as that nation tries to find its identity after overthrowing Hosni Mubarak and Mohamed Morsi. I will fill out these lines of thought in the chapters ahead.

There is much that we can learn from those who live under the steamroller of Islam right now, and I think we will need to apply those lessons soon enough. I do hope we can do more than run and hide in days to come; certainly in the years leading up to that possible panicked state we can construct a walk with Jesus that will never bend under pressure. That is, ultimately, the point of this book.

What This Book Will Not Be

Other authors will take you deep into the obscure corners of biblical prophecy, offering their interpretations of each phrase, verse, symbol, and character. I have never been a prophecy geek and am too old to transform into one now. If you are one, this is probably not the book for you. I chuckled when such geeks expressed disappointment with my first book – I never promised a verse-by-verse exposition of prophetic texts, and furthermore, I am wary of anyone who does! The symbols and lack of clarity that dominate passages in Daniel and Revelation make me hesitant to tackle a definitive interpretation of every seal, every being, every confusing time span. Were the famed seals in Revelation broken during the destruction of the temple in Jerusalem in AD 70, or have they not been broken yet? Is the millennium a literal or figurative one thousand years? Will the Church be raptured before the great tribulation, in the middle of it, or after it? Libraries are full of books that have been written to debate these questions and hundreds of others. I do not want to add to that giant genre of literature with this book.

Rather, in this book I will attempt to solidify the foundation for the case made to my first book's audience. Beyond that, the everyday headlines report movement toward God's goal – the installation of Christ's kingdom. I have always had a passion for how current events relate to God's "upper story," where He is actively working to prepare planet earth for His Son's triumphant return. I believe with all of my heart that Jesus will return within my lifetime, and I think I have the evidence to back that up as we consider the Matthew 24:14 time marker: *And this gospel of the kingdom will be preached in the whole world as a testimony to all nations, and then the end will come.*

I will again make a case that we are nearer to the fulfillment of Matthew 24:14 than you probably realize, and the phenomenal events of the Arab Spring are interweaving with the incredible progress made by the Church to disciple the nations.

Of course, the "end" to come will not always be pleasant for Christ-followers. I will take a look at this too as we examine what has occurred among Christians in the lands of the Arab Spring. I think many Westerners get a little too excited about "freedom" in these countries, not understanding that the freedom was extended to conservative Muslims who would like nothing better than to rid their lands forever of infidels. That shouldn't surprise anyone in light of Muhammad's foresight, which can be found often in the Koran from verses like these:

> *The Christians affirm that the Christ is the son of God.
> Such is the talk of their mouths: it is the kind of thing
> that unbelievers have alleged in earlier times. May they
> perish at God's hand: perverse are all their thoughts!
> They take their priests and monks as lords and the
> Christ, son of Mary also, displacing the worship of God.
> This – when they were commanded to worship one God
> only – there is no other God but He. May He be glorified
> from all that they falsely associate with Him. They seek
> to extinguish the very light of God with their utterances.
> But this God will frustrate. For He wills only the perfecting of His light, however hateful the unbelievers find it.*

It is He who has sent His messenger with guidance and the religion of truth, making it victorious over all religion, notwithstanding the hatred of those who worship plural gods. (Sura 9:30-33)

If you are reading this book on a Friday, I can guarantee you that an imam somewhere in the world is preaching on these verses as you read. These verses are one of several examples in the Koran of what Muslims await. They are discussing excerpts like this more and more as they gain power in countries both Islamic and secular. They sense too that this promised victory is imminent.

So, even though I am not fully confident in my exposition of biblical prophecy, I hope to make up for that lack with my knowledge of the Islamic heart and doctrine. I do not speak Arabic fluently (yet), so I have not ventured into the hearts of those who live in a large part of the Middle East. I have, however, spent many hours in conversation with Muslims in three communities on the continents of Africa, Europe, and Asia. I have also done a fair amount of research into Islamic documents and quizzed Muslim teachers on how they see the world and its future. It is this ear-to-the-ground perspective that I think gives me credibility as I write about the Islamic world, a viewpoint that has only been enriched by two years in the capital of Turkey, a fascinating and key country in the early twenty-first century.

I didn't predict the Arab Spring clearly, but I knew that millions of Muslim citizens around the world wanted their god in government far more than was known. In that way, they are much more like Americans than we understand. I will unpack this idea as well, to help you understand the Muslim heart better so you too can predict where this worldwide movement is headed. To some degree you only need look in the mirror and change the language from "God" to "Allah" and from

"Christian" to "Muslim" to discern what animates the hearts of god-fearing Muslims.

How could life in the West ever be so bad that people would run to the hills as Jesus said we would in the Last Days? If Muslims ever interact with Western nations from a position of strength, with access to nuclear weapons and a willingness to turn off the oil spigot in lieu of continued riches, they will not be seeking long-term peace treaties which they have to respect, nor will they allow American culture to continue unchecked in our world.

Muslims call our country "the Great Satan" not because they hate our "freedom," but because they hate the immoral culture we have spread around the globe, which they see as polluting the minds of their children – the same effect that we see and dread.

I don't believe that Muslims will ever have the numbers to conquer the U.S. from within. I think people who subscribe to that idea refuse to believe that we could ever be defeated from without because that does not look likely in 2014. But give Islamic nations a few years to organize under a powerful leader and combine their resources, from Pakistan's nuclear arsenal to Saudi Arabia's oil reserves, and we could have an extremely formidable adversary, one far more threatening than China, the current country everyone wants to focus on. If and when Islam unifies, with appropriate resources and goals much more similar to Muhammad's, then the non-Western world will resemble the great Ottoman Empire of old, which came *very* close to swallowing up Europe.

Muslims call our country "the Great Satan" not because they hate our "freedom," but because they hate the immoral culture we have spread around the globe.

I think we will be overwhelmed by an outside force comprised of Muslims ruling over subservient countries around the planet, leaving the U.S. as a kind of final course on the menu, another gift of our geography, which has served us well more than once in world history. We will be the last frontier of victory that Muhammad envisioned. I am not sure exactly what that conquest will look like. Rather, I want to focus on the fireball that is growing abroad, what it means for Christians, and how it fits into God's plan for the Last Days.

Before we celebrate the Arab Spring too vigorously, we must realize that it has led to a dark and cold Christian Winter. That season has already begun for believers in Iraq, Libya, Egypt, Tunisia, and Syria. This Christian Winter will be the true climate change of the twenty-first century for which you and I need to prepare.

By the way, I am well aware that many well-meaning Christian authors have written books just like this in years past, as they were convinced the events of their time were a precedent to Jesus' return. Those authors' books have come and gone. Their works have either deteriorated beyond recognition or are available for a penny on *Amazon.com*. This book could well join their ranks. But I believe the immense progress we have made in the spreading of the gospel, combined with the Middle East serving as a focal point in the world again, makes our time strikingly similar to the scenario painted by biblical prophecy. At this point, all I can do is ask you to weigh my arguments and decide for yourself.

I have been flattered by the praise for my first book and hope that this sequel will be a blessing to many others. I give you *Arab Spring, Christian Winter*.

CHAPTER ONE

Mohamed Bouazizi and the Last Days

Mohamed Bouazizi, the "man on fire" in Tunisia, probably never laid eyes on a Bible. He had no idea Scripture predicted a confederation of nations in the Middle East aligning against Israel in the End Times, led by a powerful central figure who hates the true God. Bouazizi would have thought we were crazy if we suggested to him that his name would be remembered forever as the man who began the Arab Spring. He would have certainly had us fitted for straitjackets if we told him that he was actually a pawn in the hand of the Christian God, needed to give Islamists the courage and hope to overthrow tyrannical governments in Egypt, Libya, Tunisia, Yemen, and other countries.

One reason why history fascinates us so much is that seemingly minor characters can trigger a reaction that changes the entire world. Do you know who Gavrilo Princip was? He was the man who assassinated the archduke of Austria-Hungary and his wife, precipitating World War I. Princip was a member of a Serbian terrorist organization, probably unknown to everyone except his family, friends, and the local police. However, his actions ignited a few horrible years involving what was considered the most brutal war in history, a conflict that re-drew the map of Europe and shaped a generation. One could even argue that "The Great War" changed the entire philosophical perspective of the Western world. Princip had no idea that his shots would change the way millions of people viewed life, but they did. Bouazizi was a similarly unknown character whose act shook the world.

Today, the Muslim world looks much more like a bloc that is ready to take on the Western world for global supremacy. The new, unchained voice of the people is openly critical of the West and its values, and the word *jihad* is heard much more often, even in the highest reaches of government. For a brief period of just one year, we got a glimpse of what a large, "modern" Islamic nation would look like under an Islamist president, as Mohamed Morsi of the formerly banned Muslim Brotherhood led Egypt. Morsi's term in office came to an abrupt end for a variety of reasons, from a lack of progress in the economic realm to his desire to overthrow the "Deep State" in Egypt. Yet, for a fascinating twelve months, we were able to witness the jihad of the Brotherhood against rulers who were not Islamic enough. That Brotherhood, still active across the Middle East and primed to gobble up more power, bases its philosophy primarily on the writings of Sayyid Qutb, one of the most influential Islamic thinkers of the twentieth century, and a man whose name you should know.[5] Even though he had been a middling leader in the movement for years, Morsi was primed to be the first elected Islamist president in history, with the prominent bruise on his forehead proving his devotion to prostrated Islamic prayer five times a day. Hmmm. Where have I read about markings on foreheads in Scripture?

The new wave of leaders after the Arab Spring is all Islamist to one degree or another, although Egypt has capped this explosion for now with the return of Abdel Fattah el-Sisi, a general, to serve as prime minister.

Bouazizi had no idea that he had triggered the fulfillment

---

5   Peter Hessler, "Arab Summer," *The New Yorker* (June 18, 2012).

of God's plan for the final years of current history, but he did. Not bad for a humble produce vendor.

On that December day in Sidi Bouzid, Bouazizi lit a match to ignite his body, and consequently, the passions of an entire region's people. In less than a single year, the Middle East was altered, a testament to the pent-up rage which Muslims in several countries had felt for decades as their basic human rights were ignored by ruthless dictators. One of the wonders of this metamorphosis is that it didn't require intervention from a Western nation to pull it off! No, it was all homegrown, as the basic human desire to be free erupted in fifteen countries across North Africa to the eastern edge of the Middle East. But where would that freedom lead? We are beginning to find out.

The notion that Islamic fundamentalist politicians would form the core of governments of Tunisia, Egypt, and Libya seemed impossible as 2010 drew to a close. What would change? What *could* change? Life was still a brutal struggle as tyrants imprisoned and killed their enemies, and ignored their citizens, building massive fortunes while their people went hungry.

I've lived in the developing world under an unresponsive government, and I can tell you that it is hard to watch the daily suffering of the average citizen, who usually wants to work and has an extremely industrious spirit, as Bouazizi did. Everywhere you look, people are hustling to make a dollar or two (literally) each day because there is zero trickle-down effect and no job creation programs. Young boys sell Kleenex on busy city streets, dodging cars to get to median strips where they can shove a few packets inside the open spaces where car windows have been rolled down. These street urchins literally risk their lives to make a few cents. Men in torn clothing push wheelbarrows on dusty outlying roads, offering to collect your garbage and take it to a landfill for pennies. Women sit in market stalls with a few shriveled peppers hoping to sell a couple and have enough to buy a bouillon cube to make their own sauce to pour on their rice that night. Government handouts? Nowhere to be seen. If you ever want to see a country without big government and people forced to rely on their own initiative, travel to the developing world and tell me again that government is inherently evil and always blocks economic progress – but I digress.

In the developing world, the government couldn't care less about the average citizen – until it comes time to pay some sort of invented tax for using a market space, pushing a wheelbarrow, or selling Kleenex.

Life Among the Mohamed Bouazizis of the World

Even though I never met Mohamed Bouazizi, I feel like I *have* met him. He reminds me of the many Muslim friends I had in Côte d'Ivoire, West Africa. Those small-time merchants formed the core group in society that I and my teammates sought to reach with the gospel of Christ. I watched those merchants struggle with a deaf government and corrupt officialdom for four years, culminating with the highly suspicious burning of the vast market in our city of one million. Hundreds of wooden stalls went up in flames in a single night as part of an inferno so loud and destructive we could hear it two miles away in my home. Have you ever *heard* a fire? It's a chilling sound that I will never forget, a roar that sounds like a stadium crowd but never stops to take a breath.

Early the next morning after the blaze, we were told of the devastation and knew that many of our personal friends' businesses were ruined. Eyewitnesses said the fire had begun simultaneously in four corners of the market, a phenomenon that is impossible without advance planning. Most people believe the flames were lit by government-backed arsonists who wanted to force the stubborn small businessmen and women to rent spaces in the new concrete municipal market that charged more than double the rent. Welcome to political policy in the developing world.

Dozens of vendors jumped into the flames that night, brothers of Bouazizi in a sense. They knew that their life savings were burned to a crisp as their inventories went up in flames or the fire destroyed the currency they had buried in their stalls, as many had. They also drew the quick conclusion that they would never get out from underneath their crushing debts, as all possibilities for profit turned into smoke. Thousands of others packed their bags the next morning and fled the city and country, returning to Mali and Burkina Faso to begin a new life far away from their creditors and a hostile government. The fire was a clear message to these Muslim immigrants: "Pay up or get out of town." Little wonder that Côte d'Ivoire exploded into civil war a couple of years later as rebels set up their headquarters in Bouaké and ruled the northern half of the country for four and a half years.[6]

Because of this experience watching small-time merchants suffer horribly, I understood Bouazizi's struggles and knew immediately why he did what he did. His action reflected the common citizen's cry of "Enough!" in reaction to the despicable treatment that the average person receives from a distant and dishonest government. Bouazizi was a hard-working man who supported his mother, uncle, and younger siblings (his father died when he was just an infant). As a vendor, he faced constant police harassment because those officers made much of their living on bribes, as many government workers do in the developing world. That's not entirely their fault; inefficient governments are often months late on payment, if the paycheck comes at all.

Perhaps you too have felt the weight of government on your small business. Maybe you too have longed for righteous

6   http://allafrica.com/stories/200212030058.html (June 27, 2013).

men and women to run your country. Part of the premise of this book is that my readers have far more in common with Islamic fundamentalists than they would ever imagine. That doesn't mean that we are cousins in the faith, but it does mean that we share many of the same desires, yet our visions of the world change shape drastically as they are funneled through our worldviews. In other words, of all people to understand Islamic fundamentalists, we evangelical Christians should be first, because both of our "tribes" long for a world where God reigns supreme and where fervent practitioners of our faith are in charge. That's precisely why true Christ-followers should never, ever be surprised by any rightward swings in the Islamic world.

Bouazizi had experienced run-ins with the police many times in his decade or so of laboring in his town's streets, a precarious existence shared by millions of earnest men and women across our planet. You can fly to one hundred countries today and find innumerable small businesspeople like him, men and women who occupy a tiny space in a market or push a cart and sell vegetables and fruits. They are known by everyone and almost universally loved as they provide a quality product every day at a fair price. Think of your mailman or, if you are old enough, of your milkman. These vendors have to maintain a pleasant outlook and be cheery with their customers, or they will be out of business quickly. Bouazizi was this type of person, by all accounts.

On the day he set himself on fire, he was told he lacked a proper permit, but he could be forgiven of this fabricated requirement if he anteed up a large-enough bribe. This cycle of harassment and bribes had run for years, to the point that he had accumulated an ongoing debt to his suppliers. On December 17, he needed to have a good day of sales to make a dent in his two-hundred-dollar debt. Think about the pressure of that sort of debt when you make only a few dollars a day. Beneath his sunny exterior, Bouazizi was stressed, a bomb waiting to explode in many ways.

The fuse was lit when he met up with a surly female municipal officer who scolded him for not having the proper permit – again – and may or may not have slapped Bouazizi, depending on which eyewitness you believe. In any case, his electronic scales were confiscated by the officer and his produce cart was tossed aside. The fact that all of this went down in public view was an extreme humiliation for Bouazizi in a shame-honor culture, which we Westerners will never fully understand. The shame cut to his heart. How would he face the public again after this latest degradation?

Day after day, city officials troll the market looking for ways they can extract bribes to pay for invented trespasses.

When he later went to the governor's office to reclaim his scales and a small measure of his personal dignity, he was ignored again, as commoners in the developing world are treated every single day. Bouazizi reportedly said, "If you will not see me, I'll burn myself." He promptly bought a gallon of gasoline, returned to the governor's office, and doused himself with it. In the middle of traffic, he let out a cry that ordinary merchants scream every day in exasperation to city officials on the take: "How do you expect me to make a living?"

As someone who tried hard to help small businesspeople in West Africa launch enterprises, I can tell you that municipal officials, and a host of other obstacles, make it nearly impossible for new businesses to succeed. Day after day, city officials troll the market looking for ways they can extract bribes to pay for invented trespasses. It is discouraging to hear from people that you sponsor telling you that yesterday someone in a uniform asked them for the equivalent of one week's profit or they would be shut down. Add the random thievery that also strikes most of these businesspeople at some time or another, and it is a wonder that any humble vendor can make a living and feed his or her family. We should all stand at attention and marvel at the perseverance and courage of the Bouazizis of the world. How could he make a living indeed?

To prove that he was a man of his word, Bouazizi lit the match at about 11:30 a.m. local time. His body was quickly covered with severe burns despite the attempts of onlookers to douse the flames. Eighteen days later, Bouazizi died, despite a visit from Tunisia's president and a typical unfulfilled promise of an airlift to France for treatment. The 90 percent of his body that was burned proved to be too much for his weary soul. I think he lost the will to live. Three days after Bouazizi's death on January 4, 2011, Tunisian President Zine El Abidine Ben Ali fled his country for fear of his life, which suddenly ended his twenty-three-year dictatorial rule. The Middle East would soon be turned on its ear.

The Suicide That Changed the World

Protests had already begun in Tunisia the day after Bouazizi's dramatic statement in the main street of Sidi Bouzid.[7] The long-dormant rage over daily humiliations like the one in Tunisia that drove a man to suicide spread to Algeria, Jordan, Egypt, and Yemen within a month, as if fuses were strung across the borders, igniting one another in a lightning-quick relay.[8] Literally millions of affected citizens of these countries gathered in huge public squares to demand the abdication of their dictators. The common phrase chanted in Arabic during the selected "days of rage" (often coinciding with Friday prayers) was, "The people want to bring down the regime."[9] Within eight short months, Tunisia, Egypt, and Libya had new governments – a stupefying

7   Lin Noueihed, "Peddler's martyrdom launched Tunisia's revolution," *Reuters UK: www.uk.reuters.com* (January 19, 2011).

8   Sudarsan Raghavan, "Inspired by Tunisia and Egypt, Yemenis join in Anti-government Protests," *The Washington Post* (January 27, 2011).

9   Uriel Abulof, "What Is the Arab Third Estate?" *Huffington Post* (March 10, 2011).

turn of events that no one could have predicted in late 2011.
Certainly no prophet arose to foretell that a vegetable salesman
would be the spark to topple governments in several countries
with administrations that had been backed by powerful mili-
taries for decades. But God had a plan.

Out went Tunisian strongman Ben Ali (twenty-three years
of iron-fisted rule), Egyptian President Hosni Mubarak (thirty
years in power), and Libyan Emperor Muammar Gaddafi (forty-
two years in power). Yemeni President Ali Abdullah Saleh
(with thirty-three years of crushing tyranny) saved his skin by
immediately calling for elections, which resulted in him being
replaced by Abd al-Rab Mansur al-Hadi in February 2012. The
"Burning Man" in Tunisia catalyzed a power shift that ended
a combined one hundred and twenty-eight years of despotism
– an unbelievable God thing. But to what end? This book will
answer that question.

Taking a cue from Saleh in Yemen, other leaders quickly
announced their immediate or eventual resignations to avoid
the danger of peasants storming their palace gates. These leaders included Sudanese President Omar al-Bashir, Iraqi Prime
Minister Nouri al-Maliki, and Kuwaiti Prime Minister Nasser
Mohammed Al-Ahmed Al-Sabah.[10] In Jordan, four governments
have been formed and dissolved under King Abdullah's rule,[11]
while the suffocating nineteen-year-old state of emergency in
Algeria was lifted in January 2012.[12]

Here is a brief rundown of other aftershocks:

• In Oman, Sultan Qaboos dismissed his ministers and

---

10   "Kuwait's Prime Minister Resigns after Protests," *BBC News: www.bbc.com*
       (November 28, 2011).
11   "Jordan King Appoints New PM, Government Quits," *Reuters: www.reuters.
       com* (February 1, 2011).
12   "Algeria's State of Emergency is Officially Lifted," *Bloomberg: www.bloom-
       berg.com* (February 24, 2011).

granted law-making power to the legislature, a novel concept in many Arab countries.[13]

- Bahrain's King Hamad has shuffled his government's leadership and released political prisoners.[14] The situation in this country is still fluid.

- Morocco's King Mohamed VI responded to widespread protests by calling for constitutional reforms and an end to corruption.[15] It remains to be seen just how transparent his rule will be.

- Even Saudi Arabia's petrified leadership caved a little, with King Abdullah holding elections in September 2011, and granting women the right to vote and serve in municipalities in 2015![16]

- Palestinian Prime Minister Salam Fayad resigned in April 2013.[17]

- Lebanon, Mauritania, Djibouti, Somalia, and Iran have all seen protests with limited effect – to this point.

Finally, the most recent ripple effect of the Arab Spring precipitated the brutal civil war in Syria, as a coalition of mostly Islamist fighters sought to boot Bashar al-Assad to the curb. This horrific three-year war continues, with the Islamist force called ISIS still controlling certain key regions of the country and on the brink of establishing a true Islamic republic at the

---

13   "Oman's Sultan Granting Lawmaking Powers to Councils," *Voice of America: www.voanews.com* (March 13, 2011).

14   "Bahrain Sacks Ministers Amid Protests," *Press TV: www.presstv.ir* (February 26, 2011).

15   "Moroccan King to Make Reforms with Constitutional Body," *Middle East Online: www.middle-east-online.com* (February 22, 2011).

16   Abeed al-Suhaimy, "Saudi Arabia Announces Municipal Elections," *Asharq al-Awsat: www.asharq-e.com* (March 23, 2011).

17   *http://www.nytimes.com/2013/04/14/world/middleeast/salam-fayyad-palestinian-prime-minister-resigns.html?src=recg&_r=1&* (June 15, 2013).

time of this writing.[18] Much to the dismay of both Western governments and many Syrians, the most pure form of Islam has outlasted other rebels in Syria to claim power in historic and formerly diverse cities such as Aleppo and Raqqah.

From coast to coast in the Muslim world (the Atlantic Ocean bordering Mauritania to the Arabian Sea off Oman), the long-squelched voice of everyman in the Middle East – a Muslim far more devout than the English-speaking, Western-educated Muslims we see interviewed so often on television – was shouting and would soon make itself heard at the ballot box. I know these people. I have spent hundreds of hours on the streets in Islamic communities talking with them. I am never surprised by their courage, their huge numbers, or their conservatism.

What the Arab Spring Revealed About the Average Muslim

The post-dictator election results, which swept many Islamist candidates into power in several countries, shocked Western observers as they realized how the "average" Muslim in the Arab world viewed the rest of the world. This enormous majority of average citizens believe that godly values matter in politics, and that the holy word of Allah should have a leading role in law and society, just as the founder of Islam wanted. What also shocked reporters was that the men in Tahrir Square in Cairo were not all uneducated simpletons calling for the Koran to function as the constitution. Stereotypes of men and women who never finished high school being duped by Islamist propaganda could not be supported by the actual events. In a flash, well-groomed men in business suits walked into Egypt's Parliament eager to advance an agenda that they had formulated over decades of involvement in the Muslim Brotherhood. The Brotherhood

---

18   *http://www.ft.com/cms/s/0/306fb482-0c41-11e4-9080-00144feabdc0. html#axzz39eXwGHHH* (August 6, 2014).

was delighted by the uprisings, because they knew they had a grassroots organization in place to make a rapid move into the power vacuum, and they did.

Sure, there were plenty of secularized young people in Tahrir who simply wanted Mubarak out and sought to raise a ruckus to break the boredom of their lives. *Not only have Christians fled the Arab Spring countries in record numbers, but they have been beaten, tortured, and killed as never before.* But all across the Middle East, long-outlawed political parties with an iron-strong Islamist worldview came out of the shadows and were swept into power by Allah-fearing citizens who were sick of the secularized elite. In short, the Middle East was not itself for decades. Dictators stemmed the tide of conservative Islam – many times backed by U.S. administrations – in exchange for cooperation in the region. Now, we are learning more and more about the true will of the people, the real worldview of the average Muslim.

Mohamed Bouazizi's death brought rapid climate change to the Arab world, where spring came in January of 2011, earlier than usual on the calendar. In some ways it was the first true spring for millions of Muslims around the world. That Arab Spring, however, has led to the commencement of a Christian Winter. Not only have Christians fled the Arab Spring countries in record numbers, but they have been beaten, tortured, and killed as never before in places where they formerly lived in a tense peace with their Muslim neighbors, from Iraq to Nigeria, and Syria to Myanmar. I believe that this Winter will deepen in the next several years, and will soon resemble the time Jesus warned about in Matthew 24:6-14:

> *You will hear of wars and rumors of wars, but see to it that you are not alarmed. Such things must happen, but the end is still to come. Nation will rise against nation, and kingdom against kingdom. There will be famines*

*and earthquakes in various places. All these are the
beginning of birth pains. Then you will be handed over
to be persecuted and put to death, and you will be hated
by all nations because of me. At that time many will
turn away from the faith and will betray and hate each
other, and many false prophets will appear and deceive
many people. Because of the increase of wickedness, the
love of most will grow cold, but the one who stands firm
to the end will be saved. And this gospel of the kingdom
will be preached in the whole world as a testimony to all
nations, and then the end will come.*

The ultimate purpose of this work is not to spout theories
or try to prove how smart I am; its true goal is to encourage my
fellow Christians to stand strong and true to Jesus no matter
what the future brings, and to lift our heads to see His coming, which I believe will be within my lifetime. I will base all
of my ideas not just on what I read in the media, but on what
I have experienced in Muslim communities over a decade's
time on three continents. Because of my extensive interactions
with average people in a variety of contexts, I believe I have an
accurate reading on the pulse of the real Islamic world, not the
one that is often presented in the news.

Even if a Christian Winter deepens, we can still find warmth
as we share our coats and work together to build a fire. I think
we will see the beauty of the Church as never before, even as
Christians around the world and throughout history have
treasured the *koinonia* that emerges when believers are heavily
outnumbered and persecuted.

Just a few years ago a fire burned Mohamed Bouazizi to death.
It set the Islamic world ablaze and Christians are fleeing to the
mountains (Matthew 24:16). The cold is coming, because when
it's early spring in one part of the world, it's late fall in another.

CHAPTER TWO

The Spread of Islamism Around the World: How and Why It Had to Happen

Americans always seem so shocked to see bearded Muslims shouting in the streets and calling for an Islamic republic in their countries. Why are we so jolted by this passion? It mirrors our own much more closely than we realize. A person who has been born into Islam and has grown up in an overwhelmingly Islamic community and country will naturally want to see a just government ruled by godly leaders who lean on Allah's word for wisdom as they direct national affairs. Does that ring a bell? Does that sound like the last political rally that *you* attended?

In the case of the Muslim citizen, he or she feels deeply in their heart that if the nation can only begin to live more closely aligned with the Koran, then Allah will bless the people and give prosperity to all, a far cry from the ruthless poverty that wears on millions of Muslims worldwide. Does that sound familiar? I think of the verse that says, *Blessed is the nation whose God is the LORD* (Psalm 33:12). Muslims feel the same way, but they substitute "Allah" for "God."

Thus, the idea that God wants to play a significant role in a given country's evolution is shared by Muslims and Christians. We Jesus-followers pray for our political leaders as 1 Timothy 2 tells us to. We do that, right? Even with a Democrat in the White House? I hope so.

Muslims hope that they will have leaders who are true Muslims, not phonies who simply pray in public and build mosques to demonstrate their piety, then embezzle millions of dollars from the national treasury and buy estates in Europe for frequent retreats. They want men who are seeking to walk in Muhammad's footsteps and who will ultimately establish *sharia* law in the country, with the Koran as the constitution, the definition of an Islamist. A modest lifestyle has long been prized by Muslims in their leaders, and their coming messiah will demonstrate that, as I detail later in this chapter.

A modest lifestyle has long been prized by Muslims.

Did the Arab Spring Help or Hurt Islamism?

How did these Islamists fare in elections once the dictators were chased out of the country or killed in public view? I will not try to match the extensive media coverage of what is transpiring in Muslim countries, but a quick look from sources that have extensive reporting experience in the region can prove instructive as I build my case that a more unified, truly Islamic world has emerged today and will continue to gain momentum tomorrow. As we take this rapid tour, I would add that the only way to know precisely what is occurring on the ground in these tumultuous countries is to be an Arabic speaker who has great access to power structures and can circulate easily within the major cities. That is impossible for one person to do, which is why no one can predict perfectly what the aftermath of the Arab Spring will be. For English speakers, the most we can do is rely on journalists who write in English and have a fairly good sense of what is occurring. This is a second-tier look at events, however, as if trying to see clearly through a distant fog hanging over these countries. But it's the best we can do.

If I had to summarize the state of many countries impacted by the Arab Spring as I write in the summer of 2014, I would characterize them as struggling in transition, with widespread violence ruling the day. The strongman has been thrown off in these nations, but when that happens, law and order break down on the local level. That is precisely what journalists and other observers are reporting in these newly "free" lands. In the capitals, politicians are fighting behind closed doors to decide who will run their countries, while on the streets in cities and towns outside the capital, various movements, gangs, and militia are enforcing whatever code of law they favor. In many cases, that is *sharia* law, through which Islamists are gripping the local populations, including Christians (more on that in chapter 3). From the ground, life usually looks worse than it did when tyrants ruled. The initial fervor of a successful rebellion has morphed into despair over lawlessness and tension.

With this general picture in mind, I want to take a particularly close look at four countries that will either help to determine the aftermath of the Arab Spring or which may have special significance in biblical prophecy. These four countries will give you a nice synopsis of where the Arab Spring will lead and how that ties into what God's Word seems to predict for the Last Days.

Tunisia

We begin with Tunisia, the land of the man who started all of this. Tunisia has traditionally been a country that has leaned more toward the West than other nations in North Africa. Its citizens see themselves as sophisticated and superior to neighboring Moroccans and Algerians. All of the Tunisian friends I had in France were sharp people who worked good jobs and sneered at the comparatively "uncultured" Algerians and Moroccans around them. They would always tell me that the brutes from other North African nations did *not* represent Muslims or Arabs well at all. Tunisians are far less apt to engage in behaviors that exacerbate the daily tension between the French and Arabs; they don't typically spit on sidewalks, they speak French well, and they often work white-collar jobs for respectable corporations. Subsequently, you will find far fewer Tunisians by percentage on the crime rolls. During my years in France, I knew of none who dealt drugs, committed petty theft, or set cars on fire. I'm sure part of this is due to Tunisia's less complicated history with France, but I also think that Tunisia often produces a different type of person than other North African countries.

I remember the guest presentation of a Tunisian friend in one of the French classes that I taught in a suburban Washington, D.C. school. She talked a lot about the Italian influence in her country, Tunisia's proximity to Europe, the many Europeans who vacationed or had even moved to Tunisia, etc. She spoke as if Tunisians were semi-Europeans due to their continual exposure to Italian television programs, their inclusion of basic Italian in their daily language, and their belief that they had developed a civilization on the foundation of ancient Carthage and Rome – a dubious assumption, at best. As she spoke, I heard very little about the cultures native to modern Tunisia or any mention of Islamic or Arab pride. It was as if this woman, a dear person, wanted to communicate to us all that she was much more like us than different from us. She overreacted to a basic insecurity, I think, as she addressed these small groups of students from wealthy homes. I think that she and many other Tunisians see themselves as inhabiting a cultural spot somewhere between North Africa and Europe; they are proud to be Tunisian but insist that they are nearly Western as well. These dignified people, many of whom are well educated and have long been more supportive of women's rights than most Islamic countries, provided a good test case for the triumph of moderate Islam after the Arab Spring, a country most likely to produce the type of society that we envision when we use the words "liberal democracy."

In short, of all the countries affected by the Arab Spring, Tunisia would be a very safe bet as the least prone to steer rightward into fanatical conservatism. Alas, many Tunisians have no desire to have a European society, evidently, and millions of them follow Islam as closely as any other Muslims in the world, according to election results, media reports, and eyewitness accounts that I have gathered.

This again proves a point that I have made repeatedly to audiences around the world: do not take the temperature of the Islamic world based on your English-speaking, university-educated friends, or on the interviewees on television who speak English and are highly educated. For every one of the people like my guest speaker friend, there are ten (at least) who did not finish high school, do not speak English, and believe that Tunisia is relatively poor because it has not obeyed Allah. There is a level of society in every Islamic country that does not often appear in the media (as in the U.S., unless you watch "Here Comes Honey Boo Boo," a documentary on Appalachia or life in the inner cities), but has made its presence known as ballot boxes have sprouted after the Arab Spring. Mohamed Bouazizi unleashed the voice of these people, not the elite English-speakers who have often been near or in power.

Michael J. Totten, a veteran journalist in the Middle East and writer for the journal *World Affairs*, recently spent time in Tunisia and noted that:

> *The Islamist Party, Ennahda, did very well in recent elections, winning 43 percent of the vote. Some of its supporters at the polls could be fairly described as Islamic moderates or mainstream religious conservatives, but the party's leader, Rachid al-Ghannouchi,*

cannot be. He praises suicide bombers who murder
Israeli civilians and the terrorist insurgency that ripped
the guts out of Iraq.[19]

It remains to be seen how much influence al-Ghannouchi
wields in months and years to come. Despite Ennahda's election gains and position as the top party in the country, only
28 percent of Tunisians recently polled expressed confidence
in the group, whose name translated means "The Revival."[20]
Praised as a "Mandela" of the Middle East for bringing together
secular leaders and their perspectives with his Islamist party,
al-Ghannouchi has also drawn criticism for his slow prosecution of those responsible for assassinating political leaders from
the left, killings that have rocked Tunisian society. I think the
West should be very, very careful about embracing this man
or heaping accolades upon him. Any man who leads a party
named "The Revival" should be wary of where that revival of
Islam will take a political party and a nation. Al-Ghannouchi
has been widely praised for removing direct references to *sharia*
law from the Tunisian constitution, but one wonders if this
was just a temporary provision in light of the stiff opposition
he and his party faced in Parliament.

No matter what the constitution says, the country faces
severe threats not only from the Salafists (an ultra-conservative
faction) within the ruling party, but from thousands of mer-
cenaries who were trained in Libya and went on to fight in the
Syrian civil war in the name of Islam. Tunisia has supplied a
"disproportionate number of fighters to the Islamist cause in
Iraq and Syria," with most of them joining ISIS now, according

---

19   Michael J. Totten, "Arab Spring or Islamist Winter?" *World Affairs Journal:*
      www.worldaffairsjournal.org (June 6, 2013).
20   *http://www.al-monitor.com/pulse/originals/2014/02/ghannouchi-tunisia-*
      islamist-nahda-washington-visit.html# (August 8, 2014).

to the Soufan Group, a security analysis firm in New York.[21] The country where many of its citizens see themselves as semi-Europeans provides an outsized number of soldiers willing to die in martyrdom for ultra-fundamentalist armies. Who would have predicted that? And a better question that I'm sure is keeping Mr. al-Ghannouchi awake at night is this: What happens when those thousands return home? You can be sure that they will push for a more widespread application of *sharia* law on the ground level, and before you know it, Tunisia will be a more conservative society than any of its neighbors, a complete reversal of culture due to the liberating effect of the Arab Spring. Tunisia is a prime case study for what I seek to convey in this book and what I have said for more than ten years – when "freedom" comes to Islamic countries, pure Islam quickly and actively rushes to the stage and insists on running the show.

Pure Islam quickly and actively rushes to the stage and insists on running the show.

Al-Ghannouchi does indeed acknowledge the very real dangers that more progressive people face in his country, from both Salafists in the streets to returning Holy War veterans.[22] I have an eyewitness report from a close friend who traveled to Tunisia recently that black-clad Islamists lead regular protests in the streets of Tunis on various issues, including women not being properly covered on Tunisia's many beaches. When these bearded men and black-chador-clad women began to shout and assemble, everyone cleared out of the area for fear of violence. There is a definite Islamist column in Tunisia that gains confidence by the day and enjoys asserting its strength on the street level, cleaning up society to make it more appealing to Allah.

Since the Arab Spring, the vibe in this country has changed

---

21   http://www.nytimes.com/2014/08/06/world/africa/tunisia-in-political-transi-tion-fears-attacks-by-citizens-radicalized-abroad.html (August 7, 2014).

22   http://www.al-monitor.com/pulse/originals/2014/02/ghannouchi-tunisia-islamist-nahda-washington-visit.html#.

drastically, according to every source I've seen. Tunisia would have been everyone's guess for the Arab Spring country where moderation would most likely win out; instead, several moderate leaders have been slaughtered and Islamists have emerged as the dominant political group and maintain a very public and vocal presence. Revival indeed.

I think a proper analysis of Tunisia is that even though we want this country to emerge as a moderate Islamic democracy that somehow mysteriously grows out of imagined Roman-Western roots, it has millions of people who are Islamists and have no desire to drink liquor, wear bikinis, or speak Italian as measures of their sophistication. It's precisely the type of country that Western journalists *want* to believe will be like their home countries, but is not; it's a place where people want to continue to go for vacation but might not be able to if the Islamists block the beaches.

Totten summarizes it this way:

> *Tunisia's urban liberalism is alive and well even if the countryside and the desert interior are more conservative and Islamist. Yet the Islamists are still more popular than any other one party. They may never take over the country, but we should take a wait-and-see approach before declaring definitively that it's springtime in Tunis.*[23]

The assassinations of prominent left-wing politicians have given Tunisia a Wild West feel and have put all liberals and moderates on edge. As Karima Bennoune, a law professor at UC Davis stated in a recent *New York Times* op-ed piece entitled "Killing the Arab Spring in Its Cradle":

> *But Ennahda itself bears much of the blame. It should be recognized, and condemned, for being the radical party that it is: a party that has created a climate*

23   Michael J. Totten, "Arab Spring or Islamist Winter?" *World Affairs Journal:* www.worldaffairsjournal.org.

of escalating fundamentalist violence that threatens the lives of liberal, left-wing and secular activists. The Western media have portrayed Ennahda as an innocuous voice of moderation, but it has been pushing for a constitution – one Mr. Brahmi vocally opposed – that would lay the foundations for a repressive Islamic state.[24]

So much for what we see as a fairly tame Islamic country producing a liberal democracy! If Tunisia can't pull it off, many observers doubt that any Islamic nation can.

Bennoune continued:

Since it attained independence from France in 1956, Tunisia has had some of the region's most progressive laws relating to women and families. Many fear that Ennahda is trying to undo those laws. Amel Grami, an intellectual historian at Manouba University, whose campus was besieged last year by Salafi activists opposed to women's equality and secular education, says the Arab Spring has 'triggered a male identity crisis' that has magnified the extreme positions taken by Islamist parties. In Tunisia, she has noted, fundamentalists have called for girls as young as 12 to don the niqab, which covers everything but the eyes. An Ennahda lawmaker has called for 'purification of the media and purification of intellectuals,' while female Ennahda deputies have urged segregation of public transportation by gender. Some Salafists have spoken of legalizing female genital mutilation, a practice largely foreign to Tunisia.[25]

As I have tried to state clearly in this chapter, the Arab

---

24   *http://www.nytimes.com/2013/07/30/opinion/killing-the-arab-spring-in-its-cradle.html?_r=0* (July 31, 2013).

25   Ibid.

Spring uncorked a bottleful of bubbly fundamentalism that had remained stopped up for decades. Once the strong man was removed in these countries, the large and aggressive fundamentalist groups leaped onto the streets to enforce their vision of Islam in the twenty-first century, which looks surprisingly similar to seventh-century Islam. These people were thrilled to have the chance to vote and elect leaders who shared their worldview.

A recent Pew Forum report on Muslims' attitudes across 40 Islamic-majority countries revealed that a whopping 56 percent of Tunisians support *sharia* law as the official legal code for their country, and an incredible 55 percent viewed Islamist parties as superior to other political groups in their nation, with an additional 28 percent saying they were at least as good. That means that 83 percent of Tunisians have a favorable impression of Islamist parties, a figure that surely shocks many long-time observers of this land.[26]

56 percent of Tunisians support sharia law.

Why does a relatively small country such as Tunisia matter? Because even though this nation is low in population, it has an importance beyond its size. It is a laboratory to see exactly where the Arab Spring will go. It is the birthplace of the Spring, obviously, and it also has a hefty slice of secularized Muslims, perhaps the greatest hope for a transition out of dictatorial rule into a Western-style democracy with huggable moderate Muslims calling the shots. The entire world is watching and wondering which way this country will turn. As a recent *Washington Post* article put it:

> Although Tunisia is a small country of 11 million people, its looming decisions on national identity, the role of religion and political organization touch on – and are

26   http://www.washingtonpost.com/blogs/worldviews/wp/2013/05/02/what-the-muslim-world-believes-on-everything-from-alcohol-to-honor-killings-in-8-maps-and-4-charts/ (October 2, 2014).

THE SPREAD OF ISLAMISM AROUND THE WORLD: HOW AND WHY IT HAD TO HAPPEN

likely to become a beacon for – the main challenges facing reformers across North Africa and the Middle East.[27]

I wonder what that "beacon" will look like when the head of the party in power makes statements like these: "All those who dare to kill the will of the people in Tunisia or in Egypt, the Tunisian street will be authorized to do what it wants with – including to shed their blood."[28]

Forgive my pessimism, but that doesn't sound very promising.

Central to the decisions on Tunisia's identity is the role of Islam in law, a key plank in Islamist politics. In the nearly two years since the new government took over, Ennahda has battled the secular minority over the role of *sharia* law in the country's constitution, a battle that must be watched in all countries of the Arab Spring. A compromise was reached that pleased neither side, stating that Tunisia's law will be based on "Islamic teachings."[29] Given that the constitution must be approved by two-thirds of the assembly representatives, observers are now predicting a delay in new elections, which might not be held until 2015.

Tunisia also needs to be closely followed because it has served as a surprising stage for a Salafist party. The Salafists, who take their name from the Arabic word for "predecessor" (*salaf*), seek to turn the clock back to the golden age of Islam, when Muhammad's earliest followers lived out the faith as it was originally intended. That means strict adherence to the Koran in all areas of life and a puritanical approach to Islam. According to some Western intelligence agencies, this is the fastest-growing philosophy and political party within Islam.[30]

---

27 *http://www.washingtonpost.com/world/tunisia-faces-political-struggle-over-islam/2013/06/16/1000670a-cdef-11e2-8845-d970ccb04497_story.html* (June 19, 2013).

28 "Killing the Arab Spring in Its Cradle," *Worldnews: www.wn.com.*

29 "Tunisia Faces Political Struggle Over Islam," *Washington Post: www.washingtonpost.com.*

30 *http://www.aina.org/news/20120416150547.htm* (June 9, 2013).

Let me write that sentence in another way: Western intelligence agencies say that the fastest-growing political party in the Islamic world seeks to turn the clock back to AD 610. Digest that truth for a while then look into the future with me.

We should never be surprised if the voice of pure Islam is loud and large. These millions of devout Muslims have been persecuted for their faith for decades and are reveling in their ability to express themselves in a variety of ways. Restrictions on them have included imprisonment of conservative clerics, restrictions on wearing the hijab head covering by women, and an avowed separation of mosque and state as laws are made. Muslims around the world have chafed under these limits. Scores of women have wanted to wear their hijab as a sign of modesty when attending university classes or entering a government building, for example. Millions more have longed for the Koran to play a larger role in law making, not a smaller one.

After decades of subservience to secularists in government, these religious Muslims are laser-focused on their goals for change in their countries and believe with all of their heart that they are building just societies, cultures that reflect what Allah has long desired. Eventually, they hope that these model Islamic societies will multiply all around the world, a necessary precursor for the final day of judgment. Their motivations run deeper than the merely political, and they are energized in an almost supernatural way to see their way of life instituted in Tunisia and around the world. These new movements spring from the heart and soul, not the head, and are one reason why I believe they will have a large say in all governments of the Arab Spring. As the majority Islamists shout in the streets of Tunis, "The people are Muslim. We won't surrender!"[31]

As of this writing, Ennahda continues to steer a coalition

---

31 http://www.nytimes.com/2013/03/13/world/africa/tunis-journal-a-front-row-seat-for-an-uprising.html?_r=0 (July 15, 2013).

government that includes two secular parties and recently named twelve independent "technocrats" to important positions in government, hoping to prove that Islamists can share power with experts who do not have their worldview. Who knows? Perhaps Tunisia will somehow combine Islamism with secularism, leaving the actual execution of governmental functions to men and women trained for those jobs, no matter what their religious or political persuasions are. Eventually, people grow tired of governments that cannot deliver economic progress, a weakness that many Islamic governments have had (see Iran for details). The primary issues facing the government appear to be the timing of new elections and two nettlesome articles in the constitution that refer to Islam's direct role in governance.[32]

The U.S. shares a keen interest in which way the Tunisian revolution will swing, having sustained an attack on its embassy in September 2012, which left four dead. Such trouble was, again, unheard of during the Ben Ali years. Beji Caid el Essebsi, a major leader of the secularists who hope to win power in the next elections, provided a tidy summary of the tug-of-war in the birthplace of the Arab Spring: "We are for a secular state, while they [Ennahda] are for a religious state. The bottom line is that we stand for two different kinds of society."[33] For now, the government is walking a tightrope – trying to nullify the efforts of the most violent Salafists in the country who go by the name Ansar al-Sharia ("Partisans of Sharia"), while seeking to out-maneuver the secularists and build Tunisia on pure Islam. It will be a fascinating laboratory to observe over the next few years. For now, Islamism continues to be the people's choice, and if they can keep the country afloat economically, they will gain even more power and push for their cultural agenda as well.

32 *http://www.guardian.co.uk/world/2013/jul/12/egypt-upheaval-region-mohamed-morsi* (July 15, 2013).

33 http://www.aina.org/news/20120416150547.htm.

Egypt

Speaking of intriguing experiments in democracy, Egypt continues to defy conventional wisdom, from the triumph of a member of the Muslim Brotherhood in the first elections in

Out of camera view, a massive political organization was ready to pounce into action.

2012, to the recent coup that deposed President Mohamed Morsi and the deadly attacks on Morsi supporters by the military, now in bed with liberal and secular parties. The July 22, 2013, *Time* magazine cover said it all: "World's Best Protestors/World's Worst Democrats" written over a picture of thousands gathered in Tahrir Square.

What fool would try to predict what will happen in this chaotic country that plays a role in biblical prophecy? Egypt has drawn many of the headlines in the Arab Spring because of its enormous population (more than eighty million), its position as a key Arab state, and the soft spot many Westerners have for it because they enjoyed seeing the Pyramids and other stunning sites while vacationing there. We all thought that we saw a bit of ourselves in the Egyptian uprising. It looked a little like Woodstock, as young people in jeans climbed onto tanks, almost like putting flowers into gun barrels. And gosh, the entire movement was spawned by a Facebook page – how much like us![34]

Yet, out of camera view, a massive political organization called the Muslim Brotherhood was ready to pounce into action and lift the country out of its secular rut and squarely onto the high ground of what the prophet Muhammad intended for the Muslim community. This party was joined by the Salafists here too, as in Tunisia. Combined, the Muslim Brotherhood (40 percent) and the Salafist parties (25 percent) won two-thirds of

---

34   See *Revolution 2.0: The Power of the People is Greater Than the People in Power: A Memoir* by Wael Ghonim, Mariner Books, 2013. This is a fantastic book about the power of social media and the role it played in Egypt's dramatic changes.

the votes in the first round of parliamentary elections in 2012.[35] Think about this: Two out of every three Egyptians want their country to be an Islamic republic. Is there any doubt now that this brand of Islam will mold this vital country in years to come?

Yet the one-third of voters who did not see their will imposed on the new Parliament continued to clamor for change that involved less Islam and more secular democracy, or at least a more generous sharing of power by whatever party's president was in charge. Secularists were joined, albeit reluctantly, by the very conservative Nour Party, which also felt impotent as Morsi tried to position himself above the courts and ram through a constitution heavy on Islamist doctrine that was never supported by a majority of Egyptians. For now, as that *Time* magazine cover story said, "For many Egyptians, protest equals democracy. Popular as it was, the coup sets a precedent for transferring power not by the ballot box but by the mob."[36]

I gained a fascinating perspective on what caused Morsi's overthrow when I attended a seminar on the aborted revolution in Egypt at a local university. On the panel that night were Egyptian students and businesspeople who provided eyewitness accounts of the overthrow of Mubarak, and later, Morsi. One engineer helped me understand why an Islamist could be run out of the presidency despite the backing of a majority of citizens. It was not only Egyptian impatience with economic gains, which were negligible under Morsi, but it was also the Islamic Brotherhood's desire to cleanse all of the country's institutions of secular army rule, from military headquarters, to courts, to police. In political science terms, this is often called "Deep State" and is most commonly used in reference to Turkey (more on that in chapter 5). Morsi took on Deep State and lost; he overstepped his bounds in seeking to not only re-frame the

---

35   Michael J. Totten, "Arab Spring or Islamist Winter?" *World Affairs Journal:* *www.worldaffairsjournal.org.*

36   Karl Vick, "Street Rule," *Time: www.topics.time.com* (July 22, 2013).

constitution, but to install Islamists in the courts, the police, and the military. The Egyptian military was not at all prepared for that change, and Morsi was not a deft-enough politician to overhaul an entire society. Once I understood that Morsi had taken on Deep State, I was able to digest how Islamism faced a quick reversal in Egypt and reconcile that event with my thesis: Islamism will prevail wherever "free" Islamic societies emerge. One of the rebel movement's leaders stated it best in summarizing why Egypt was not quite ready for an Islamist president: "Let's be honest, the army has controlled the country for centuries."[37]

That control has extended to all areas of Egyptian life. The military quickly took control of most media outlets, pulling the plug on four private television stations that were run by Islamists, a very discouraging development in a part of the world in which Westerners have long wanted governments to grasp the importance of a free press, as well as freedom of religion and other basic human rights.[38] Another of those basic rights – the right to life – has also been threatened as military forces have slammed into pro-Morsi sit-in camps, firing live ammunition and doing whatever it takes to get these new "rebels" off the streets. At least two hundred and possibly three hundred people were killed in the second wave of attacks on these somewhat peaceful demonstrators in August 2013.[39] I write "somewhat" peaceful protestors because it appears that pro-Morsi crowds torched churches in at least four cities in response to the attack of the military in Cairo, a troubling trend that I will focus on in chapter 3.[40]

On the other side, the supposedly neutral government of

37   Ibid.
38   http://www.reuters.com/article/2013/07/07/us-egypt-protests-media-idUS-BRE96607H20130707 (July 15, 2013).
39   http://news.yahoo.com/police-storm-protest-camps-192-dead-across-egypt-195053079.html (August 14, 2013).
40   Ibid.

al-Sisi, who was elected in May 2014, has reignited a vicious crackdown on the Islamic Brotherhood, which I think will reinvigorate that huge party in Egypt. Even secular Egyptians who rejoiced over Morsi's ouster have expressed "a growing unease at the scale and severity of a crackdown on his now-outlawed Muslim Brotherhood."[41] Part of that attempt to crush the Brotherhood has been the arrest of thousands of its leaders and members, many thrown into prison for dubious charges of "terrorism." The country waits to see if the top Brotherhood leaders will be executed for their supposed crimes. As of this writing, the Islamic religious leader of the country, the Grand Mufti, has not approved of the first wave of executions, with more than a thousand others under the same sentence. "Western governments and human rights groups … have condemned the hurried way in which the courts have reached such serious verdicts."[42]

For now, the military in Egypt has again seized the reins of this enormous and important country, but don't be surprised if a second "Spring" bursts forth in the next few years as the people again rise up to protest authoritarian rule. Will the Brotherhood again lead the country? Just in case, let's take a brief look at the mindset of a clear majority of Egypt (52 percent voted for Morsi) and speculate very carefully and tentatively on how this mass of citizens could impact its country and the world's future. The Pew Forum report mentioned earlier in regard to Tunisia shows that 91 percent of Egyptians believe that Islamist parties are better than or as good as secular parties in their country.[43] Attempts to outlaw and crush the Muslim

---

41   http://www.reuters.com/article/2014/08/07/us-egypt-courts-badie-idUSK-BN0G70ZJ0140807 (August 7, 2014).

42   Ibid.

43   http://www.washingtonpost.com/blogs/worldviews/wp/2013/05/02/what-the-muslim-world-believes-on-everything-from-alcohol-to-honor-killings-in-8-maps-and-4-charts/ (October 2, 2014).

Brotherhood are akin to trying to cap an explosive liquid with a flimsy cork.

Before the Morsi government was overthrown, we got a few glimpses into Islamist thinking as the new regime took charge. When asked why the U.S. gave $250 million in aid to Egypt in the spring of 2013, one Salafist leader said it constituted a "poll tax" on Americans to soothe the Muslim Brotherhood. "They pay so that we will let them be," said Khaled Said, the official spokesman for the Salafi Front.[44] He compared the U.S. gift to the Islamic jizya tax that it habitually imposed on infidels, a tariff that our country must pay to honor the Egyptian government and have the right to pass through its airspace and waters. "They must pay reparations for destroying our country and the Islamic nation – them and others in the West – so we will agree to cooperate with them," he added. We appreciate this explanation, Mr. Said!

I could write a lot of analysis about this quote, but let it serve as an example of the confidence of this new Islamist bloc. They believe that the West's time is over and that it is only a matter of years before Islam asserts itself as the one true religion. Said's comments reveal this mindset, which is habitually underreported in the West because journalists do not understand it. They are bamboozled by these types of quotes because they do not understand Islamic history, and they seek to be so politically correct that such quotes cannot be repeated and analyzed.

Before he was ousted, Morsi gave a brief preview of what Islamic countries will look like when they become truly Islamic. One key policy area to keep an eye on in Arab Spring countries and other Islamic republics is the national attitude towards alcohol. Morsi pushed for higher taxes to discourage consumption, while Salafist politicians called for an all-out

44   http://www.washingtontimes.com/news/2013/mar/28/egyptian-cleric-says-american-aid-mandatory-tax/?page=all (June 6, 2013).

ban. As in Tunisia, look for a gradual move to the right in Egypt as time passes. I think that the cold-blooded killing of Muslim Brotherhood supporters by the army (estimates of the dead range from seventy-two to more than two hundred)[45] will create a new sympathy for the Brotherhood that will lead to them gaining even more numbers and some sort of political compensation for their losses. In other words, the backlash to the recent killings (at the time of this writing) will create a rebound effect that will have the Brotherhood seen in a sympathetic, victimized light.

The huge question that lingers over Egypt's future is how the central role which the military traditionally plays will morph, as the country tries to behave as a democracy and respect the results of the ballot box. Like many armies in Middle Eastern countries, Egypt's has defended secularism for decades, and it was quick to flex its muscle when it appeared that the Morsi government had no interest in sharing power with secular parties that also won seats in Parliament.

What will happen tomorrow? It's impossible to say, but Totten's words are instructive. After spending time in-country recently, he said, "The country is, as far as I can tell, the most Islamicized place in the world after Saudi Arabia. It used to be oriented more toward the Mediterranean, as Tunisia still is, but that was more than a half century ago."[46]

Would any of us Bible believers think that Egypt would *not* play a key role in the era before Jesus' return? Where will this country of more than eighty million people go in the next few years? I think it will again take its place as a powerful arch-enemy of Israel, even as it was in the time of the Exodus. The difference is that pagans are not running the land of the Nile now – the conservative Muslim people on the street are. But

---

45   http://www.ynetnews.com/articles/0,7340,L-4410101,00.html (July 31, 2013).
46   Ibid.

no matter how many people assemble in squares to show off their popularity and prove to Egypt and the world that they are the majority, the 2012 election results indicate that two-thirds of Egypt is not secularist or liberal. How long will it take that majority to gain permanent power and direct the country towards an Islamist constitution and state? Your guess is as good as mine. I do believe the majority will rule, but there will be many more hiccups along the way. Whatever happens, it will be interesting and important. As Christian Whiton, a former State Department senior adviser said, Egypt's bumpy ride to democratic rule is "the most titanic political contest of our era."[47]

If I had to guess, I think that Egypt will continue to convulse until a competent politician with a conservative bent can make enough allowances and kick-start the economy to keep the secularists and the poor from constantly rioting. I believe the election results from 2012 show clearly that the majority of Egyptians lean Islamist, but they will not yet vote blindly for these candidates if the economy stays stuck in reverse. Look for more trouble in Egypt, but don't cross your fingers hoping for a moderate government. The tide has turned and will not recede.

As veteran CNN International Correspondent Ben Wedeman, a man who has covered Egypt for years, said after Morsi's ouster, "Despite the fact that many people are fantasizing that this is the end of the Islamist movement," the country will continue to "have to deal with the Brotherhood either as a political movement or underground movement."[48] What could transpire is the suppression of the Muslim Brotherhood again, which could lead to an eventual revival of the movement that would throw off restraint and crush any enemies in the path of Islamism. Christiane Amanpour had these thoughts right after the coup: *One of the great triumphs of the Arab Spring was that*

---

47   http://www.cnn.com/2013/07/10/world/meast/egypt-whats-next/?hpt=hp_c2
        (July 15, 2013).
48   Ibid.

it showed Islamists who were prepared to come into the political process and accept the democratic path forward rather than the violent jihadi future that Osama bin Laden and al-Qaeda were espousing. But if they are kicked to the curb even after winning elections, the future could grow very perilous. As Amanpour asked, "What are you going to tell Islamists: that democracy is for everybody except them?"[49] That could well be the question of the next half-decade!

Egypt merits your interest even if you grow bored with Middle Eastern politics.

By the way, how would you like to be an official with the U.S. State Department as all of this shakes out? Your choices are: 1) Endorse a president who comes from the notorious Muslim Brotherhood, or 2) Endorse a military coup that nullified the type of democratic elections the U.S. has pushed for (in rhetoric at least) for decades. As the French say, "Quel choix!"

Egypt merits your interest even if you grow bored with Middle Eastern politics, because many prophecy experts see that country as playing a key role in the End Times. One popular theory has Egypt filling the slot of the *king of the South* talked about in Daniel 11, a king who will clash with the *king of the North* in an epic battle just before the return of Messiah Jesus.[50] Other students of prophecy find today's tumultuous events predicted in Isaiah 19 and other passages, although Egypt has not exactly been tranquil for many years between Isaiah's time and now, and we could cite several *cruel master*[s] and *fierce king*[s] (Isaiah 19:4) who have ruled that land over the past few thousand years.

We could apply those verses to any number of kingdoms soon after Isaiah – Persian, Greek, Turk, French, etc. It is a little

---

49   Ibid.
50   *http://www.wnd.com/2012/11/is-egypts-president-fulfilling-biblical-prophecy/* (June 7, 2013). This article is written by Joel Richardson, an extremely astute observer of modern events as they relate to biblical prophecy. See *www.joel-strumpet.com* for more.

hard for me to make the leap from Isaiah talking about Egyptian leaders consulting mediums and spiritists, to Islamists, who eschew folk Islam, at least officially. Perhaps President Morsi and his cabinet had shamans at every meeting, but I think if you look at Isaiah's prophecy objectively, you have to admit that this chapter could well have been fulfilled long ago. You should also be hesitant to equate an Islamist government with *the wise counselors of Pharaoh* in verse 11 and others.

Can we call a truce between prophecy pundits and simply conclude that Egypt is an extremely important nation in both Scripture and the Arab World, and that God will shake it, along with all of the other nations, just before Christ's return? That is very safe ground, and I don't think anyone would question that Egypt will play a crucial role in the final alliance against Israel. I would submit that the changes in its government and leadership needed to play an aggressively hostile role against Israel, and will re-surface perhaps in a form more Islamist than even Morsi.

I will let the prophecy students fight it out over when Isaiah 19 was fulfilled, or if it has yet to be fulfilled. Likewise for Daniel 11, which chronicles an ongoing war between the kingdoms of the North and South, with the northern king emerging victorious. Again, some prophecy "scholars" find today's events in that chapter, and they could well be correct, although I don't see too many cities under siege entered by ramps in modern warfare (v. 15) – one of many difficulties I have in applying all of Daniel 11 to 2013.

I will stick with my thesis that I offered in my first book: the lands covered by all prophecies concerning the Last Days are in the Middle East and areas just on its edge, and those countries are almost 100 percent Islamic, making Islam's role in the final decades of time as we know it a foregone conclusion. There's too much disagreement on the details of prophecy for anyone to say they are sure. I also think that the many points of contention, combined with the attention-seeking teachers of Scripture who want to one-up each other with fearless predictions, greatly weaken our case with the unbelieving world.

Need proof? When Harold Camping predicted the end of the world for May 21, 2011, my students in Turkey knew about it before I did. When that day came and went, they took the occasion to ridicule Christianity. That's why I will not name any specific dates or even offer any potential years for the fulfillment of God's plan. In today's cyber-sphere, any outrageous predictions that draw attention are beamed around the world in a millisecond, and billions of people mock the sources of those predictions when they don't come true. Anyone want to read more Mayan prophecy, for instance? I didn't think so. We need to calm down in our specific, highly detailed prophecy interpretations so that when the Last Days do kick in and people are scrambling for understanding, they will come to us because we've preserved our credibility by not getting too whacky with our forecasts.

Even if I can't tell you precisely how today's events can be found in scriptural prophecy, I can tell you that Egypt is the Arab world's most populous nation and should be closely watched for that reason alone. Add to that the use of Egypt's name in many biblical prophecies, and you have another reason to track developments there with attention.

Libya

Libya fascinates us because we followed the mad antics of Muammar Gaddafi for so long and delighted in his downfall. He always seemed a bit off his rocker, with his wild outfits, outrageous statements, and ruthless suppression of his people. We felt sorry for the people of Libya – for good reason. Gaddafi was a lot of fun to make sport of, but didn't we all feel a little bit of a pang when we saw him begging for mercy as he was being beaten to death? His downfall was swift and brutal, stunning in its totality. Overnight, Libya went from a police state to a giant country being ruled by a variety of factions.

Gaddafi had once said that Islam should rule "from India to Spain," yet he did little to advance that mission, focusing on personal wealth and absolute control rather than

Look for a man who lives simply and seems to live for jihad, not palaces or fancy cars.

jihad. Gaddafi was in many ways the exact type of leader that devout Muslims despise: they give the appearance of devotion to Allah but behind closed doors are far more interested in power and material wealth. That's not what the average Muslim wants in a leader. Nor is it what Americans want in a president, is it?

Recall, if you are old enough, the adoration that the Ayatollah Khomeini had in Iran when he returned to rule in 1979. Did you ever wonder why he was so revered? A large part of his appeal was his simplicity, his total disregard for fancy clothing or other trappings of wealth. This is the kind of leader that Muslims long for, and the messiah al-Mahdi will be famed for his devotion to equally distributing wealth in his kingdom, among other qualities.[51] So, when you are looking for an Antichrist-type figure in current and future history, look for a man who lives simply and seems to live for jihad, not palaces or fancy cars. Gaddafi, Saddam Hussein, and other rulers arouse a particularly vehement anger among the Allah-fearing Muslims in the Middle East, so we should not have been too surprised by the horrible treatment they received in their final days.

Libya should attract our attention for more than the Gaddafi sideshows and crazy quotes ("Democracy means permanent rule" is one of my personal favorites!), or involvement in terrorism (Gaddafi was said to have personally approved the bombing

51   http://www.al-islam.org/an-overview-of-mahdis-government-najimuddin-tabasi/21.htm (July 31, 2013).

of Pan Am Flight 103 over Lockerbie, Scotland, among other attacks).[52] It should bear scrutiny for more than the Benghazi controversy, where four Americans were killed when a militia stormed the U.S. embassy there. Libya is one of the few Middle Eastern countries called by name in scriptural prophecy. Even though it does not have the size, wealth, or influence of Egypt or Iran, it crops up repeatedly as prophets attempt to give us a glimpse into the Last Days.

For now, the chaos of filling a post-Gaddafi power vacuum has drawn interest from reporters all over the world. Many predict sectarian clashes that will leave the country awash in blood as it decides what it will be. As Totten notes in an opinion voiced by many observers:

> The country is awash with guns and battle-hardened militiamen. Every conceivable political faction – from liberals and moderates to tribal leaders and radical Islamists – has supporters willing to pull the trigger for what they believe in. Even al-Qaeda has a presence in Tripoli and Benghazi ... everything from this point forward must go exactly right for Libya to emerge as anything like a stable democracy.[53]

Thus, a "stable democracy" seems to be an elusive entity in many of these countries after the Arab Spring. It's one thing to revolt, protest, and join a rebel army, but it's another to actually govern. The latest reports from the ground indicate intense battles among dozens of rival militias, all of whom are well armed. The jihadist group Ansar al-Sharia, based in Benghazi, has gained a slight upper hand in the battles, but many wonder what sort of country will be left once the fighting stops.[54]

---

52 http://www.nbcnews.com/id/41940239/ns/us_news-security/t/no-question-gadhafi-ordered-pan-am-bombing-ex-cia-official-says/ (July 31, 2013).

53 Michael J. Totten, "Arab Spring or Islamist Winter? *World Affairs Journal: www.worldaffairsjournal.org.*

54 http://www.theguardian.com/world/2014/aug/04/-sp-middle-east-politics-2014-egypt-syria-palestine-iraq-gaza, (August 7, 2014).

Tens of thousands of Libyans have fled to neighboring African countries, while others who had returned after the Arab Spring are journeying back to their adopted countries for fear of their own lives.[55] This economic and intellectual drain of resources will severely hurt Libya in the short run.

Events have turned so bad that most countries have closed their embassies and shuttled their citizens out of Libya. I have contact with a businessman in-country who recently wrote to me and said that he too was forced to leave Libya because of the daily violence around him. Trust me, if this guy left Libya, it must be unlivable right now for anyone not wanting to join an armed side. Here is how he described the country he loved:

> The past nine months have been extremely challenging as we experienced our once relatively safe country slipping into anarchy and chaos. Kidnappings, car bombs, nightly gunfire and fireworks, car-jackings, murders, robberies and assassinations became almost everyday events. … It just became too dangerous for down-to-earth Westerners like us to remain there any longer. … It will take many big miracles for this country not to turn into another Syria or Iraq or Somalia.[56]

Libya has seen its Islamist sympathizers rush to the fore of leadership as strongly as in any other Arab Spring nation. As I've stated repeatedly in this book, that should surprise no one. The most recent victories for the Muslim Brotherhood in Libya have seen one of its leaders, Nuri Sahmain, elected president of the National Congress under the Justice and Construction Party flag. This party has continued to gain momentum since elections in 2012, when it won only 10 percent of the vote. Since

---

55   Here is an excellent article about a prominent businessman packing it up in Libya after hoping the overthrow of Kaddafi would bring a prosperous new day: *http://www.businessweek.com/articles/2014-08-07/libya-waste-fraud-erase-billions-in-national-wealth* (August 7, 2014).

56   Personal email received 7/28/14.

that time, it has drawn independent politicians to its banner like nails to a magnet, forming the strongest bloc in the infant government, probably even outpacing its popular support.[57]

Currently, two men claim to be the prime minister, and no solution to their dispute looms on the horizon because the country's top court ruled the May 4, 2014 elections "unconstitutional" due to such deep controversy over its procedures and outcome. Sitting Prime Minister Abdullah al-Thinni refused to cede power to Ahmed Maiteg, the choice of Islamists and Muslim Brotherhood supporters. Maiteg has accepted the court's ruling for now, and the entire country awaits new elections that should clarify the political picture soon.[58]

The chief conflict in Libya appears to be between new government forces fighting back against Islamist militias to determine the future direction of the country. As one political analyst knowledgeable about Libya's current chaos has said, "It is a regional conflict over the survival of the Muslim Brotherhood."[59]

The world watches with keen interest because Libya is a huge supplier of oil to many Western nations, and billions of dollars from that export are on the line. Traditionally, Libya has pumped 10 percent of the oil imported by Western countries, but now that production has "cratered," according to observers, with exports cut nearly in half, a disruption to the world supply that could eventually affect prices worldwide.[60] The international airport at Tripoli has been shut down as planes burn on the tarmac. A huge fuel tank burns endlessly in Tripoli. No one truly knows who's in charge. Meanwhile, Libya continues

---

57 http://www.guardian.co.uk/world/2013/jul/12/ egypt-upheaval-region-mohamed-morsi.

58 http://www.economist.com/blogs/pomegranate/2014/06/libyan-politics (August 7, 2014).

59 http://www.bbc.com/news/world-africa-28418925 (August 7, 2014).

60 http://www.businessinsider.com/libyas-oil-sector-is-in-freefall-2014-8?utm_ source=feedburner&utm_medium= feed&utm_campaign=Feed percent3A+b usinessinsider+(Business+Insider) (August 7, 2014).

to serve as a channel for arms that often wind up in jihadist hands in Mali, Syria, and other countries. In fact, Libya could end up being a very convenient pipeline for jihadist causes all over Africa and the Middle East, a distinction that anyone rooting for Libya's government would weep about.[61]

In the near future, whoever ends up leading this shaky group of rival tribes will willingly participate in a band of nations intent on destroying Israel. Libya is called *Put* in Ezekiel 38 and is identified as a member nation in an alliance against Israel in the *future years* (Ezekiel 38:8). Put might also have included part of Algeria and Tunisia, according to the first-century historian Flavius Josephus. It should certainly stun you that Ezekiel mentions this part of the world so clearly and prominently a full twenty-six hundred years ago!

Put will join *Gog and Magog*, Iran, Turkey, and other nations to *advance against my people Israel like a cloud that covers the land* (Ezekiel 38:16) until God Himself reacts and destroys this coalition. As in other cases with biblical prophecy, some interpreters use Libya's frequent interaction with Russia to prove that Gog and Magog refer to Russia, and expound a theory of a European power producing the Antichrist. More recent commentators have said Gog and Magog are actually Turkey. Do you see why I do not want to enter the fray when the Bible is not clear? I prefer to concentrate on what *is* clear as we look at what prophecy and the news website headlines say.

In addition to focusing on the fearsome alliance that will invade Israel and trying to figure out what each name equates to on today's map, don't miss the awesome power of God as He defends His people and glorifies Himself. Oh, how I pray that many of the Muslims hell-bent on killing Jews will surrender to Yahweh as He flexes His muscle on that day!

An earthquake, pestilence, floods, hail, fire, brimstone – arms

---

61   *http://www.securitycouncilreport.org/monthly-forecast/2013-01/libya_2.php*
(July 16, 2013).

that not even nuclear weapons can match – will be employed by God to glorify Himself, as He says in Ezekiel 39:7: *I will make known my holy name among my people Israel. … and the nations will know that I the LORD am the Holy One in Israel.* May they truly know, and may they know long before this battle, I pray.

How far away are we from this titanic battle as Islamist leaders bolster their political position in Tunisia, Libya, Turkey, Iran, and other countries? Can you understand why I, and others, write books like this with special urgency? The type of Jew-hating leaders that needed to rise to the top of power in these biblical nations were imprisoned or killed before the Arab Spring. Not only were leaders suppressed, but even the average Muslim who tried to fervently exercise his faith was thrown in jail, a crackdown on fundamentalists that only fueled the rage that burst forth after the Arab Spring. For example, I have an eyewitness who told me that any men showing up for early prayers at the mosque were immediately imprisoned for six months under Gaddafi, who feared Islamists more than any other faction in his country.[62]

Sure, people like Gaddafi gave lip service to hating Israel, but he and others did little about it. Even those who do something about it, such as Hamas and Hezbollah, are limited in strength and technical skill. This final coalition will have far more manpower, zeal, and weaponry than any league that we've seen to this point.

Libya is actually called by name in Daniel 11, where in verse 43 we read that *Libyans and Cushites* will be in submission to the Antichrist as he expands his reign. Thus, Libya's participation in the final drive to overrun Israel will be both of its own will and not. Libyans will act as conscripted soldiers and a vassal state in the great kingdom of the Antichrist.[63]

---

62 Based on conversation with businessman who lives in Tripoli, summer 2013.
63 *http://flashtrafficblog.wordpress.com/2011/02/28/bible-prophecy-and-the-future-of-libya/* (July 1, 2013).

Syria

Syria, Syria, Syria. This nation is even more key than you might realize, given that many Muslims believe Jesus will descend into Damascus when He returns to assist al-Mahdi, and the region is mentioned frequently in scriptural prophecy. Do you really think that the rule of President Assad will survive the Arab Spring wave over the long term? Thanks to heavy backing from Iran and Hezbollah, Assad's army has limited rebel advances and has re-taken several key cities, including Aleppo. Assad has not, however, been able to crush the rebel forces entirely, and those groups, with ISIS taking the lead, continue to rule many regions.

Americans have been loath to urge our country's leaders to support the rebels as they have read about and seen reports on their composition. Many of the militias are hard-core Islamists and some even have ties to al-Qaeda.[64] No one really knows what type of government these diverse groups would form if they did come to power; the Sunni-Shiite split is also pronounced in the country as Hezbollah and other groups support Assad to keep Sunnis from overrunning the minorities if they sweep into power. Assad's sect, called the Alawites, makes up only about 12 percent of the population, for example. They are on the short list for extermination or expulsion if and when the regime falls. They will be vigorously persecuted not only for having produced Assad and his father, but for being "infidels." God only knows what will happen to the nation's Christian, Kurd, and Druze minorities; I fear the worst. As one veteran reporter who recently spent time in Syria said, "The sectarian monster nevertheless stalks the country again. The future will

---

64 For one of many outstanding articles from reporters embedded with the rebels in Syria, see: *http://www.newyorker.com/reporting/2013/04/29/130429fa_fact_mogelson* (August 1, 2013).

be a grim one if that monster isn't locked up and quickly, if and whenever the government finally meets its demise."[65]

Syria draws a lot of attention from Christians for several reasons. It has a historical community of Christians that have lived in the country since the birth of the early church; it borders Israel and has always been considered a vital source of "stability" in the region; and it figures in biblical prophecy, with the prediction of the destruction of Damascus drawing the most scrutiny lately from biblical commentators. Isaiah 17 is a passage that is being discussed all over the Internet as prophecy analysts see biblical mention of the civil war in Syria. Verse 1 kicks off that chapter with this vision: *See, Damascus will no longer be a city but will become a heap of ruins.* The destruction of this city is notable because it is recognized by most historians as the world's longest constantly inhabited city, which makes its decimation a truly historic event and a sign of God's seriousness in leveling the pride of man in the End Times. Whether or not the razing of Damascus will occur during this current civil war remains to be seen, and whether that will be the last time it is demolished is also open to conjecture. I'm not sure I'm willing to agree that Isaiah 17:1 is being fulfilled as I write.

> *The future will be a grim one if that monster isn't locked up and quickly.*

No one can deny the importance of Damascus in Middle Eastern politics, however. It serves as a host for terrorist groups Hamas and Hezbollah, both of which have had members living in Damascus for decades. Syria would be a logical launch pad for any military actions against Israel, one reason why the U.S. has been slow to arm the Islamist rebels in the country. Imagine how much vigilance would be necessary to keep an eye on Islamists in charge of a country bordering Israel. Think

---

65   Michael J. Totten, "Arab Spring or Islamist Winter? *World Affairs Journal:* www.worldaffairsjournal.org.

about the ramifications of that. Of course, the same can be said of Egypt on Israel's southern border if and when Islamists regain power there.

Some commentators believe Syria also shows up in Ezekiel 38 and 39 as part of the Gog-Magog alliance, as well as in Amos 1:3-5, where God says He will *not relent* (regarding Damascus) for its *three sins … even for four*. Some commentators point to Syria's involvement in the 1948, 1967, and 1973 wars with Israel as the three sins mentioned in Amos 1, with the fourth still to come in the End Times.[66] Some commentators see this final flattening of Damascus as part of a larger war with Israel, which is predicted in several places in the Old Testament. This huge battle, which involves modern-day Jordan as well, will spill over into Syria's borders and lead to Damascus's erasure as a city. Jeremiah 49:23-27 clearly discusses Damascus's downfall with language almost identical to the Amos passage:

> *Damascus has become feeble, she has turned to flee and panic has gripped her; anguish and pain have seized her, pain like that of a woman in labor. Surely, her young men will fall in the streets; all her soldiers will be silenced in that day, declares the LORD Almighty. I will set fire to the walls of Damascus;* (vv. 24, 26-27a)

There is much debate over whether some of these prophecies have already been fulfilled or have yet to be realized. Many scholars run with the "dual fulfillment" interpretation of the passages mentioned above, opining that Damascus was indeed overrun by Assyria in AD 732, but that the prophecies will have a second fulfillment in the End Times, that the city has been overrun in the past but never completely flattened, something

---

66 See *http://www.raptureforums.com/IsraelMiddleEast/damascussyriaandisaiah17.cfm* as an example of this school of thought of prophecy (July 10, 2013).

that will occur only in the Last Days.[67] Books have been written on this topic, but I don't want to add to that library right now.

Let's just say that: 1) Syria figures prominently in biblical prophecy; 2) Damascus draws repeated mention and is one of the most important cities in the world if you have a Judeo-Christian worldview; and 3) Damascus also is a key city in Islamic prophecy.

Now, with those three simple, difficult-to-debate points in front of you, do you think it's any accident that even Americans are discussing Syria constantly and trying to figure out what role the West should take in Syria? Do you think that is a coincidence?

As you ponder those questions, don't forget to pray for the people of this country who have suffered so much. As I write in the summer of 2014, the number of deaths has topped 160,000 with another 2.7 million fleeing the country. Another 3.8 million have been displaced in-country, either without a roof over their heads due to their homes and apartments being destroyed by the war, or having left the virtual prisons that their homes had become, when they were afraid to walk out and stray into the path of a sniper on one side of the conflict or another.[68] Popular author Joel Rosenberg, in an interview regarding his latest bestseller *Damascus Countdown*, calls the conflict one in which "demonic forces" have been unleashed in a virtual "genocide."[69] He also warned that the war could easily spill over into Lebanon and Jordan, completely destabilizing the region. Perhaps the Arab Spring will spill over into nations that have been untouched to this point, such as Jordan, leaving the

---

67 Look at sites like these for detailed analyses of Syria in prophecy: *http://www.prophecydepot.net/2013/syria-and-damascus-in-bible-prophecy/* (August 1, 2013).

68 *http://www.huffingtonpost.com/2014/05/19/syria-war-death-toll_n_5353021.html* (August 7, 2014).

69 *http://blogs.cbn.com/stakelbeckonterror/archive/2013/03/19/stakelbeck-on-terror-show-joel-rosenbergs-damascus-countdown.aspx* (July 15, 2013).

region completely Islamist as this brand of Islam that is willing to fight and die sweeps across the Middle East. What countries will fall next? Saudi Arabia? Iraq?

Syria has also drawn special attention from intelligence services around the world, because as the conflict there drags on, Islamist fighters from around the world are flooding into the region, creating a new haven for these guerillas, many of whom associate themselves with al-Qaeda. Some analysts have called this new Wild West for armed Islamist gangs "one of the biggest terrorist threats in the world today."[70]

More than six thousand of these men willing to die for jihad in suicide bombings have poured into Syria over the past year or so, a rate far higher than the number who ventured to Iraq after the U.S. invasion there. Their willingness to kill themselves as part of the battle has earned them widespread praise, as this tactic has provided the tipping point in key battles.

Many of these new, future martyrs have joined the famed al-Nusra Front, which has gained a reputation for fierceness and effectiveness as part of the rebel contingent. Others have latched on to ISIS. Again, I ask you if you find it unusual that these zealots determined to build an Islamic state have been drawn to Damascus, as if by a magnet. Do you not see how the daily headlines prove the veracity of your Bible?

Long-time bad man Ayman al-Zawahri has had frequent contact with the al-Nusra Front, because al-Qaeda views Syria as a new refuge for its armed members who want to carry out glorious missions for Allah worldwide. One leader of this new coalition of Islamist rebels cautioned against anyone thinking that toppling the Assad regime was this group's only goal, mentioning a desire to strike a blow for Allah in Russia, Shiite

---

70   http://www.nytimes.com/2013/08/09/world/middleeast/as-foreign-fighters-flood-syria-fears-of-a-new-extremist-haven.html?nl=todaysheadlines&emc=edit_th_20130809&_r=0 (August 14, 2013).

Iran, and other places. "We have one enemy," he said, "and we should fight this enemy as one front and on different fronts."[71]

Eyewitnesses to the conflict in rebel-held zones also report that the Islamists are enforcing *sharia* law wherever they are in control, harassing women into more modest outfits and forcing men to pray five times a day, as well as kidnapping and imprisoning liberal activists. After one recent victory, a Chechen commander who journeyed to Syria to join the fray laid out his vision for a Syria free from tyranny: "Everyone is free in his house but not free in public to break God's law. The *sharia* law is the best justice, not the Western democracy, which gives us bad regimes like Assad's."[72]

These Islamists will not proceed cautiously as Assad did.

As in many other countries in the Arab Spring, I would not bet against the Islamists, long term. Assad's forces were able to halt their incursion with the generous backing of Iran and Hezbollah, but they have not been able to completely evict this movement, which will grow as it is given time. ISIS and other Islamist militias believe most deeply in their cause and are more willing to fight and die for their vision of a country and world under the unfiltered reign of Allah. That is why I think they will eventually play a key role in Syria's future, which again sets up the Middle East perfectly for a final, momentous conflict with Israel and the West, much like Scripture describes.

These Islamists will not proceed cautiously as Assad did, protecting their power and wealth while giving lip service to hatred for Israel and love for Islam. No. These men do not live cautiously or to protect their assets, of which they have few. They are bold, brazen, and sold out to their cause, much as I am for the Lord Jesus Christ!

They will attack Israel soon after combining and organizing their forces all over the Middle East, and then ask questions,

71   Ibid.
72   Ibid.

if at all. If you think that region of the world is a hotbed now, you haven't seen anything yet. This is why the Arab Spring had to erupt into full bloom. God is preparing that region for a battle of stark contrasts, a fierce war that the prophets had difficulty describing due to the bloodshed. This is ultimately why Islamism had to spread through the sensitive band linking Iran to Morocco. God is not surprised or alarmed, and we should not be either.

CHAPTER THREE

What the Arab Spring
Means for Christians

In all the excitement as the Muslim world tasted freedom for
the first time, one group of people was almost universally
ignored, even though their future instantly changed too:
Christians living in these overwhelmingly Islamic countries.
As was demonstrated in the previous chapter, the "freedom"
we Westerners so covet and have pushed as the answer to all of
man's problems is rapidly turning into oppression for millions
of citizens in Arab Spring countries, the result of unabashed
Islamic rule. But where has that left our brothers and sisters
in Christ?

The focus of this chapter will be an overview of the widespread persecution of Christians in countries of the Arab Spring,
again examining briefly the nations of Egypt, Libya, Syria, and
Tunisia. Numerous outstanding websites document the daily
persecution of Christians worldwide, and I note them below,[73]
so this chapter will merely give you a flavor of how that persecution has greatly intensified since the events of early 2011.

As any of us who have interacted with someone claiming Christianity is a "Western" or "white man's" religion can
tell you, we have to restrain our laughter when we share with
people who throw such terms around that Christianity was,
in fact, begun by a Jewish man in the Middle East, and it grew

---

73   See, among others, www.persecution.org, www.opendoorsusa.org, www.ray-
     mondibrahim.com, www.persecution.com, www.persecutionblog.com, www.
     prisoneralert.com, www.christianfreedom.org, and www.christianitytoday.com.

rapidly there. Today, Christians comprise just 4 percent of the population in the Middle East and North Africa, a higher number than you might realize, but still a long way from its prominence fourteen centuries ago. In fact, the shrinkage of the Christian community has accelerated greatly in the past century. In the early twentieth century, the Middle East was still 20 percent Christian.[74]

Muslims try to make the argument that Christianity's near death in the Middle East proves the truth of Islam being the final, most accurate revelation from God. Some Christian preachers focus on the letters in Revelation 2 and 3, saying the early churches were not faithful, thus they had their lampstands removed by God. That might be true, but to the historian, the nearly complete Islamization of this region is due more to killings, threats, and a clear role as second-class citizens that have caused millions of Christians to leave the region. In other words, before we spiritualize this nearly complete ethno-religious cleansing, we must recognize that to the neutral observer, it has much more to do with Muslim bullying than a lack of "faithfulness" on the part of those seven churches, and all in cities that can be found in modern Turkey.[75] This is why that region has the fewest number of Christians of any in the world (thirteen million), and the smallest share of the population, according to the Pew Forum on Religion and Public Life.[76]

Is it lukewarmness leading to churches being snuffed out? Not so sure about that.

Is it lukewarmness leading to churches being snuffed out? Not so sure about that. What is the timetable for lampstand removal

---

74   http://www.thecommentator.com/article/2251/christians_the_forgotten_vic-tims_of_the_arab_spring (July 13, 2013).

75   See Bat Ye'or's excellent book *The Decline of Eastern Christianity Under Islam: From Jihad to Dhimmitude: Seventh-Twentieth Century* (Fairleigh Dickinson Press, 1996), for details on the historic squeezing of Christians under Muslim rule in the Middle East.

76   http://usatoday30.usatoday.com/news/religion/story/2012-01-30/arab-spring-christians/52894182/1 (June 7, 2013).

then, for instance? I can think of many American churches that are tepid in their witness, yet they are still around because our government protects religious groups and buildings of all types. What I *am* sure about is that Islam, even "tolerant" Islam, has never historically treated Christians as equal citizens when it has been the majority religion. We are seeing historic patterns repeat today, as again the Middle East is emptied of Christians.

Iraq: A Preview of How Christians Will Be Treated

This trend of newly empowered Muslims harassing Christians began in Iraq after, of course, the overthrow of Sadaam Hussein, which was supposed to make Iraq a Western-style democracy complete with religious freedom for all. What happened instead was targeted killings of Christians, especially in 2006-07, and the tragic decline of a Christian community that can trace its history back two thousand years. At one time, a million Christians lived in Iraq, with many observers believing they were the most protected Christ-followers in the Middle East under Hussein, a nominal Muslim at best. Today, fewer than one hundred and fifty thousand remain, with entire towns being vacated as ISIS rebels continue to spread their terror.[77] In some majority Christian neighborhoods of Baghdad, life has come to an almost complete stop as believers have fled, depleting the population in the Dura quarter from one hundred and fifty thousand to just two thousand, for instance. The conditions have gotten so bad in that neighborhood that the seven churches there have only two priests to guide the Assyrian, Chaldean, and Syriac Christians.[78] We will see similar trends

---

77   http://www.theguardian.com/world/2014/aug/07/isis-offensive-iraq-christian-exodus (August 8, 2014).

78   http://news.yahoo.com/flight-iraq-christians-resumes-amid-surge-unrest-044850189.html (November 21, 2013).

in Egypt, Libya, Tunisia, and Syria, among other countries, as every believer who can get out, will get out. We would too!

Ghaffar Hussain, a counterterrorism expert, has written about the situation for Christians in these Arab Spring countries:

> This shouldn't come as a surprise to the prudent observer. Iraq was a precursor in that it illustrated what happens in the Middle East when a tyrannical dictator is overthrown and a power vacuum is created. In Iraq we saw the emergence of jihadism, sectarian strife, and political in-fighting: three problems that are often inter-connected and feed off one another. The result, as far as the country's Christians are concerned, was an increase in abductions, torture, bombings, killings, and forced conversions. A number of senior Christian priests were also abducted and beheaded.[79]

As I edit this chapter, my daily news feed is filled with headlines about ISIS giving Iraqi Christians a simple choice with two or three options:

- Convert to Islam.

- Remain a Christian but pay an exorbitant tax (practiced throughout the history of Islam as Muslims conquer new territory).

- Remain a Christian and be beheaded.

Don't ever forget the concept of power when you think about how Muslims of all types behave. When they sense they have total control with no checks and balances forcing them to respect religious minorities, they give the clear, historical choice that ISIS is giving to non-Muslims in Iraq, as seen during the summer of 2014. Even secular news sources acknowledge this as a choice with historical precedent, dating back to the seventh

79   http://www.thecommentator.com/article/2251/
      christians_the_forgotten_victims_of_the_arab_spring.

century.[80] Mosul, where the new caliphate was proclaimed by ISIS, has seen its Christian population shrink from a healthy one hundred thousand a decade ago to two hundred now.[81]

We again see Iraq as a laboratory for what occurs when the purest of Muslims gain control of an area with followers of Jesus in it. True, all non-Muslims have been similarly persecuted, but Christians being the most numerous in the region are most affected. Even though the videos and photos are horrific, some of us are glad that the world is finally coming to understand what Islamists do when they are in charge. The persecution of Christians worldwide has been a horribly underreported story for decades. Now it is finally being beamed into our living rooms and onto our Facebook pages.

One bright spot as a result of Christians leaving their ancestral lands in Iraq is that some are fleeing to more stable, but equally Islamic areas. Thus, churches are beginning to spring up in northern Iraq, in the region known as Kurdistan.[82] Part of the displacement of Christians in the Middle East during the last decade resembles the dispersal of the early church after Stephen's stoning in Acts 8. His martyrdom resulted in the gospel spreading to places not previously penetrated, as hundreds of Gentile congregations sprang up in the first century. God always brings beauty out of tragedy, often behind the headlines, but His greatness in that way does not diminish the very real suffering Christians are enduring in lands where Islamists have been newly emboldened.

When Cohabitation Crumbles

I have not lived in Iraq, Tunisia, or Egypt, but I have lived in

---

80   *http://www.reuters.com/article/2014/07/18/us-iraq-security-christians-idUSK-BN0FN29J20140718* (August 8, 2014).

81   Ibid.

82   *http://www.thecommentator.com/article/2251/ christians_the_forgotten_victims_of_the_arab_spring.*

communities where Muslims and Christians live side by side in a tenuous peace. The idea of armed conflict along religious lines is never too far from anyone's mind, with Christians fearing Muslims will change their understanding of jihad and start the ethnic cleansing in the courtyards they share. Sometimes this division falls along political lines as well, as it did in Côte d'Ivoire, where I lived for four years in a majority Islamic city. The rebels who started driving out other ethnic groups from the city I lived in, Bouaké, did not use the word "jihad" often in their successful fight, but there was no mistaking that the rebels were nearly 100 percent Islamic. Many were people from groups that had immigrated from Mali and Burkina Faso.

These Muslim Julas (to use the general term) endured corrupt political rule for decades in Côte d'Ivoire that shut them out from power and eliminated their candidates from even running for office because of their heritage. When the Ivoirian government ruled in advance of the presidential election of 2000 that all eligible presidential candidates had to have two parents born within Côte d'Ivoire's borders – thus barring popular Jula candidate Alassane Outtara – the mutiny began, in 1999, the year after my departure. Many people asked me if I could see the civil war coming. Indeed I could, especially when one Jula friend sat on my porch in 1998 and asked if I could obtain arms from the U.S. government to help the rebels. He warned me, ominously, that a revolution was being planned and would certainly be carried out if Outtara was disallowed as a candidate. He was right.

Côte d'Ivoire had rapidly split into two countries by the fall of 2002. As an eyewitness to these fault lines of a society, I can tell you that in this case, religion was a secondary motivation. However, according to everyone who lives in the countries of the Arab Spring and in other hot spots in the Middle East, it is a primary divider.

Even when a secular government keeps religious groups from killing each other over their differing views of God and His will, there are many other forms of forced conversions of Christians in Muslim areas. In Côte d'Ivoire, for example, I heard several eyewitness accounts of believers moving into Bouaké and having to live with *It is at least as bad as we can imagine.* Muslim relatives. They were quickly told that if they wanted to have access to their uncle's foodstuffs and find a job, they had to renounce Christianity and convert to Islam. Judging from the number of people who moved into my city every month, I would guess that dozens were forced into Islam, in a "secular" country.

Now, with secular governments swept from power in several Muslim countries, you can imagine what it is like to be a Christian in Egypt, Libya, Syria, and Tunisia today. It is at least as bad as we can imagine, although we get very limited reporting on this topic, which always puzzles me. How does reporting on the massive persecution of *any* group reveal politically incorrect bias? It's a shame that only conservative think tanks, a few missions groups, and precious few other sources have typically reported on this major story in recent years.

The New Era for Christians in the Middle East

As the Open Doors World Watch List reveals, the nations affected by the Arab Spring have all jumped up the list of countries least friendly to Christians. The Open Doors organization, a group of activists who support persecuted Christians around the world, moved Syria from thirty-sixth place to third place on its most recent list, with Libya advancing several spots to thirteenth place, and Egypt jumping up this ranking as well in its 2013 report. The irony of how this occurred is not lost on some commentators:

The report also indicates that every Muslim nation that the U.S. has helped 'liberate,' including during the 'Arab Spring,' has become significantly worse for Christians and other minorities. Previously moderate Syria is now ranked the third-worst nation in the world in which to be Christian, Iraq fourth, Afghanistan fifth, and Libya 13th. All four receive the worst designation in the ranking process: 'extreme persecution.' Three of these countries – Iraq, Afghanistan, and Libya – were 'liberated' in part thanks to U.S. forces, while in the fourth, Syria, the U.S. is actively sponsoring 'freedom fighters' against the regime. Many of these 'freedom fighters' have been responsible for any number of atrocities – including massacres, beheadings, and the crucifixion of Christians, and others.[83]

Maronite Bishop Samir Mazloum of Lebanon provided an insightful comment as this list was discussed:

Today, Christians of the Middle East risk not only their rights but their lives. The Arab Spring in Egypt made life of Christians harder, but Syrian Christians suffer even more. They are now an easy target for terrorists. Moreover, people in Syria are being brainwashed that Christians were never important for the country and a mono-nation and mono-religion model is being promoted. These ideas contradict our entire history.[84]

Bishop Mazloum certainly has enough familiarity with Islamic history and law to know that pure Islam always seeks "mono-nations" with a "mono-religion model." The Arab Spring opened the door to this ideal. We will begin to see more of the

---

83   http://www.gatestoneinstitute.org/4312/muslim-persecution-christians-january (August 8, 2014).

84   http://english.ruvr.ru/2013_01_14/Persecution-of-Christians-natural-effect-of-the-Arab-Spring (June 7, 2013).

same ethnic cleansing that horrifies us, which we have seen throughout history.

I am struck most by the bishop's last line: *These ideas contradict our entire history.* Whenever we attempt an analysis of a given area and do not actually live there, it's best to hear from people who have lived there their entire lives. Someone like Bishop Mazloum has a historical perspective that we lack. He would have no problem saying the Middle East is entering an unprecedented time of religious conflict, and the new context is a result of the Arab Spring – which is one of my main points in this book. "Conflict" is not even a strong enough word, because we are talking about widespread death and millions of Christian refugees fleeing their homelands. In short, it sounds a lot like Matthew 24, where Jesus advised His followers to run to the hills. I am submitting that this Scripture is being fulfilled as I write.

Nathan Smith, a New Zealand journalist who has been keeping an eye on the Middle East for years, published several insightful comments on what life is like for Christians in the Middle East in his column "Christian Minority Tensions Follow Arab Spring":

> As the dust partially settles over the Middle East ... and
> new governments try to move past the turmoil of the
> past few years, the so-called Arab Spring is still exposing
> deep and raw ethnic tensions. The fallen governments
> in Egypt, Libya, Iraq and – soon perhaps – Syria, were
> for many minorities comparatively benign in comparison to today's states. Strongmen dictators Muammar
> Gaddafi of Libya and Egyptian Hosni Mubarak at least
> ruled their countries with a firm rule, providing some
> protection to these groups. Now, as once-maligned
> Sunni Islamic groups move into the halls of power, those

*minorities are feeling less welcome in their own homes
and cities.*[85]

As I wrote in my first book, Christians and other minorities
in these Islamic countries were equal in a way with Muslims:
ALL groups were squashed under the thumb of the dictators.
This is why I cautioned Americans all over the country as I
spoke in churches that we should be careful what we wish for
as we grew excited about the "liberation" of Iraq. Now we are
seeing what happens when the strongman is overthrown, for
better or for worse. Once that ruling power is gone, the most
energetic and organized groups rush into the vacuum created.
In these Muslim countries, they have been the Islamists, not
the moderates.

Smith continues:

> *Christians have faced steadily diminishing protection by
> Cairo since the dictator Mubarak was ousted. The cen-
> tral story running through the Middle East is of Islamist
> groups who feel emboldened by the sweeping success of
> the Arab Spring. Without dictators to protect minority
> groups, many of the larger Islamist political movements
> are taking the opportunity to begin the latest phase of
> religious warfare with all the passion that comes from
> years of simmering tension. Political leaders from
> Egypt to Syria will be of little help for persecuted Coptic
> Christians. If pressured to choose between ethnic groups,
> the new governments are more likely to associate with
> powerful Islamist movements, leaving Christians at the
> mercy of religious vigilantism and militancy.*[86]

That is quite well stated by an educated observer, and Smith's
prediction that the new governments in these countries would

---

85 *http://www.nbr.co.nz/article/christian-minority-tensions-follow-arab-spring-
    weekend-review-ns-137836* (June 7, 2013).

86 Ibid.

bow to Islamist pressure has proven true. Christians are more vulnerable than ever to hostilities from their neighbors, to which government authorities have increasingly turned a blind eye. This is truly one of the most heartbreaking and, I repeat, underreported stories in modern times.

Smith concludes with another prediction that has been right on the mark:

> In this light, it is no wonder these Christians are leaving the Middle East in droves. But it will be the region which ultimately suffers. Many of these people leave with human capital of education and ideas, along with real material goods. Once the dust truly settles in this broken part of the world, it might be culturally far less dynamic. It certainly will not be a progressive and prosperous home to a melting pot of communities.[87]

Here then is a little-discussed consequence of the Arab Spring in these countries and its resulting free-for-all. As Christians are imprisoned, tortured, killed, and many others flee, the loss of diversity in these countries weakens their overall societal health. In many of these nations, Christians have risen to top leadership positions, and without them, the quality of life for all will be affected.

Oren Dorrell and Sarah Lynch of *USA Today* have added to the good, but all-too-rare, reporting on the plight of Christians in the remade Middle East. Here is an excerpt of a recent article they wrote on this topic:

> The Arab Spring uprisings that toppled secular dictatorships have unleashed long-suppressed freedoms that have allowed Islamic parties to gain a share of political power they have been denied for decades. Their rise is creating near-panic among ancient Christian

---

87   Ibid.

communities that dot the Muslim world and predate
Islam by centuries.[88]

Their report went on to detail near-vacant Christian neighborhoods in Cairo, the fears of Tunisia's twenty-two thousand
Catholics, and Libyan believers' worries of living under an army
whose leader, Abdul Hakim Belhaj, led an Islamic militia with
ties to al-Qaeda.

Dorrell and Lynch went on to remind the world that the
last church open to the public in Afghanistan was demolished
recently, and widespread bombings of churches and assassinations of priests in Iraq have plagued that country for years,
drastically thinning the Christian population.

The article moved on to new fronts for Christian fear, such
as Syria, where kidnappings, rape, and murder are terrorizing
the Christian community. The report's summary offered little
hope for the future, in what again, I believe, is a preview of
what will take place around the world:

> *Many had hoped for better in an Arab movement that*
> *proponents said was about replacing tyrannies with*
> *democracies. 'The outlook is grim,' said John Eibner,*
> *CEO of the California-based human rights group*
> *Christian Solidarity International. 'If the current trajec-*
> *tory continues, it's reasonable to think that within a*
> *generation these (Christian) communities will not look*
> *like functioning communities,' Eibner said. 'They'll*
> *look more like the once-flourishing Jewish communities*
> *across the Arab world that are all but gone.*[89]

Eibner is right on target, and his prediction is accurate.
Within a generation, or sooner, Christian communities will
be a mere memory in the countries of the Arab Spring, and
probably beyond. Churches that are left will be turned into

88 "Arab Spring Christians," *USA Today.*
89 Ibid.

mosques or made into museums. Christian neighborhoods will be desolate or filled with Muslims. The brain drain in these countries will range from noticeable to substantial. Perhaps then there will be more news coverage, when a de facto genocide has been completed.

To Be Christian in Egypt

We turn first to Egypt, the Arab Spring country with the highest percentage of Christians – at least until the Arab Spring began! Many believers in Jesus are not waiting for the flames of persecution to flare before making every effort to get out of town. They are leaving before being arrested, tortured, or killed. As Richard Spencer recently reported in the British newspaper *The Telegraph*, "hundreds of thousands of Coptic Christians have departed from Egypt since the new government came to power there in 2011."[90] As Father Mina Adel, priest of the Church of Two Saints in Alexandria, was quoted, "Most of our people are afraid. Not a few are leaving – for America, Canada and Australia. Dozens of families from this church alone are trying to go too."[91] Mina's church gained notoriety on New Year's Eve 2010 when it was the site of a car bomb that killed twenty-three.

"Salafis meet Christian girls in the street and order them to cover their hair," Mina added. "Sometimes they hit them when they refuse." This atmosphere of daily trouble has arisen as the newest Egyptian constitution was passed last year. As one church leader in Cairo said, "With the new constitution, the new laws that are expected, and the majority in parliament, I don't believe we can be treated on an equal basis." A dozen families have left his church, and forty or fifty other friends have applied to leave the country, he added.[92]

---

90   *http://www.telegraph.co.uk/news/worldnews/africaandindianocean/egypt/9798777/
      Egypts-Coptic-Christians-fleeing-country-after-Islamist-takeover.html* (June 7, 2013).

91   Ibid.

92   Ibid.

If you are a Coptic church planter in the U.S., the news is all good. The two Coptic churches that existed in the U.S. in the 1970s have mushroomed into 200 and counting, as at least 40,000 Coptics poured into the U.S. in 2011 alone. "We are trying to accommodate all of the new arrivals," said Atef Yacoub, a member of the Washington D.C. area's Coptic community. "People are coming and staying by applying for asylum or seeking employment visas."[93]

Could this be a preview of what the world will look like in the next decade, with Christians moving into non-Muslim countries as Islamists push them into various corners of *Where is the world outrage?* the world? Yes, I think that is precisely what will happen, making the world a much more polarized and segmented place, ripe for direct confrontation, and ready for the final war to end all wars.

I'm happy for those Coptic brothers and sisters who were able to get out of Egypt alive, but I know they left behind six million others who need our prayer support daily. Now that former president Mohamed Morsi has been pushed out of power, it will be interesting to see if the new military government will protect Christians better than his government did. Early returns are not promising. An outburst of violence against Christians and church buildings was not halted by the new government in the summer and fall of 2013. Government leaders saw this spasm of violence as a minor price to pay for Morsi supporters to vent their anger. The government's position is understandable, though not commendable. If it defended the Christians, it could further enrage Islamists, but if it did not defend the Christians and their buildings, then only a sliver of the population – 10 percent and shrinking – would howl in protest.

Where is the world outrage? What would the reaction in the press be if seventy, or more, mosques were destroyed in the

---

93   Ibid.

WHAT THE ARAB SPRING MEANS FOR CHRISTIANS

U.S.? That story would last for days and possibly weeks. Yet little has been said about the widespread destruction of churches in Egypt in direct response to Morsi's overthrow on July 3, spanning the months of July through September of 2013.

According to one journalist on the scene, at least seventy-four churches were attacked, burned, and desecrated. Christians in the country, fearing the new government will turn against them as well, or the Muslim Brotherhood will storm back into power, have said little after seeing their historic structures decimated and several people killed in the violence. Typically, a few believers stand in the church doors trying to stave off a thousand or more enraged Islamists who want to eliminate all vestiges of Christianity in Egypt. "Copts are terrified to speak," one prominent newspaper editor noted. Their silence doesn't really matter. Police have publicly stated that they do not intend to go after any vandals. "Our job is not to protect churches," one police colonel stated clearly. Perhaps that is why a grand total of one person has been arrested in connection with attacks that involved tens of thousands of Islamists.[94]

This attitude, by the way, is one of the chief indicators of a new era in Egypt, because at least when churches were burned down in the past, the Mubarak government did try to apprehend the perpetrators. Now, nothing is done, whether the government is Islamist under Morsi or "secular" under the military leader General Abdel Fatteh el-Sisi (as it is at the time of this writing).

Those Morsi supporters are said to be using the attacks as a bargaining chip with the new government, promising to halt them once they are allowed to have a greater voice in the Egyptian government, and perhaps call a truly fair and free election in coming months.[95] How would you like to be a pawn

---

94   *http://www.miamiherald.com/incoming/article1957487.html*
     (November 18, 2013).

95   Ibid.

in a political struggle based solely on your religion? That is what our Christian brothers and sisters are living with daily in Egypt.

Whether Islamists ultimately rule Egypt, or they make trouble for Christians while the secular government stands by, it's not hard to envision an Egypt with only smoldering ruins where approximately two thousand steeples once stood. Will we believe a new era has begun if two thousand fires burn down every church in Egypt? That would serve as strong evidence of a definitively new era in Middle Eastern history.

Christians might also hesitate to protest because the last time they made their voices heard en masse was October 2012, when they organized in downtown Cairo to decry the lack of government investigation of attacks on churches. The military attacked these demonstrators and seventeen of them were run down and killed by military vehicles, according to Human Rights Watch.[96]

I think it's interesting that people around the world want to hail the Egyptian military for being "neutral" no matter who is in power, that this branch of Egyptian society is the only one worthy of the people's trust. I wonder what the families of the seventeen killed in October 2012 think of the military's "neutrality," let alone the families of hundreds of Morsi supporters who have been slain by that same "neutral" military.

An interesting reaction to watch for as Christians flee Egypt – dodging the burning embers and bricks of their own churches – will be how the U.S. government responds to these first rumblings of ethnic cleansing. The future of Christians and other minorities in the countries of the Arab Spring "is a huge issue most vividly seen in Egypt and the Copts," said California Rep. Howard Berman, ranking democrat on the House Foreign Affairs Committee. "Their treatment of Christians and other

---

96   "Arab Spring Christians," *USA Today.*

minorities is a 'red line' that will affect future aid," he added.[97] Will it? What is the "red line"? How many must be killed? How many churches destroyed?

The Morsi government moved quickly to tighten the noose around the neck of the Christian community, and el-Sisi's government has done little yet to reverse the attacks and harassment after the Arab Spring. Persecution of Christians, which admittedly occurred under Mubarak, was at least deemed somewhat illegal, and certainly outside of the legal framework. The difference post-Mubarak is that Christians are being persecuted *within* the law.

The entire matter of blasphemy offers a good case study for the harassment of Christians in Arab Spring countries. Any expression even hinting at a disapproval of Islam is considered blasphemy and illegal. The small slice of Egyptian society that can be characterized as liberal – writers, activists, comedians – has been impacted by this new law, but Christians seem to have been singled out for prosecution for this crime. Many have been sent to prison already under this extremely dubious charge. Making it even more flimsy, children are accusing adults of this crime, including their Christian teachers.[98]

Two thoughts popped into my mind as I have examined some of these blasphemy cases. First, any time you have children turning in adults and helping to send them to prison for their words alone, you have a cultural upset that reminds me of China's Cultural Revolution. Second, why is it that Christians are always accused of "hate crimes" and blasphemy? All Western societies need to be extremely careful about hate speech legislation. It can quickly be turned on any group that is out of favor at that moment.

---

97   http://www.huffingtonpost.com/2012/02/01/middle-east-christians-arab-spring_n_1248026.html (June 7, 2013).

98   http://www.csmonitor.com/World/Middle-East/2013/0522/In-Brotherhood-s-Egypt-blasphemy-charges-against-Christians-surge-ahead (November 22, 2013).

I won't go into extensive detail about these blasphemy cases,[99] but some have reached even into the U.S., with Egyptian courts attempting to have American pastors extradited to face execution in connection with YouTube videos and other supposedly inflammatory media, including postings of cartoons on Facebook that can be interpreted as offensive to Muslims. That might get your house and the neighbors' houses burned down in Egypt, as it did for Gamal Abud Massud. Other cases against Egyptians include downloads of an amateurish movie about the life of Muhammad (actually available on Islamic sites!) and even arguments over religion with Muslims, as huge mobs demand death sentences.[100]

The truth is, it is illegal to even converse about Islam in Egypt today, unless you say it is indeed God's final revelation through the prophet Muhammad. Any other opinion can land you in court, facing sentences of up to ten years in prison. I wonder what evangelism courses look like in Coptic churches! Saint Francis of Assisi's famous counsel on winning people to Jesus by only using words "if necessary" is probably applicable right now in Egypt.

It would be no exaggeration to say that Muslims have begun a reign of terror in Egypt. There is no representation for Coptic Christians accused of crimes; churches are targeted by car bombs; and believers face daily threats of rape, torture, and intimidation. May the Lord help you if you are a Coptic woman in Egypt today. Several have been raped by Muslim mobs, and daily harassment has been reported in several cities. One typical incident involved two women in traditional Islamic dress, who clipped off the hair of two unveiled Christian women on

---

99   See Raymond Ibrahim's fine book, *Crucified Again: Exposing Islam's New War on Christians* (Washington, D.C.: Regnery Publishing, 2013) for more detail.

100   *http://www.csmonitor.com/World/Middle-East/2013/0522/ In-Brotherhood-s-Egypt-blasphemy-charges-against-Christians-surge-ahead.*

the subway in Cairo, according to an Egyptian newspaper. It was the third such incident in two months, late in 2011.

Does anyone else begin to see images flashing in their minds of old newsreels showing Jews sporting armbands and being restricted to live and work in certain ghettos of European cities? What was the next step after daily public humiliation of the Jews in Germany? I think you know. This, friends, is what our brothers and sisters in the faith face every day of their *What was the next step after daily public humiliation of the Jews in Germany?* lives in the countries of the Arab Spring. Think of it. Any day you take the subway you could get your hair cut off; any time you head to church, you could face a mob burning it down; and any discussion you get into about the superiority of Jesus over Muhammad could lead to a ten-year prison sentence. Pause for a moment right now and intercede for our spiritual relatives in the Middle East as you try to imagine a daily life like theirs.

Raymond Ibrahim, a Shillman Fellow at the David Horowitz Freedom Center, an Associate Fellow at the Middle East Forum, and author of *Crucified Again: Exposing Islam's New War on Christians,* offers in summary: "Christian persecution in Egypt has gone from being a common, though technically illegal, phenomenon, to being widespread, and now legal."[101]

Shaul Gabbay, University of Denver professor of International Studies, adds, "There is no longer anything to hold them [Muslims] back. The floodgates are open. It will only get worse. The Muslim Brotherhood ... is moving forward to implement its ideology – which is that Christians are supposed to become Muslims."[102]

One new Islamist group, called Jihad al-Kufr ("jihad against unbelievers") has sought to live out this theology by targeting priests and telling them to convert or die. One widely reported

101 Ibid.
102 http://www.foxnews.com/world/2013/03/26/
egyptian-mosque-turned-into-house-torture-for-christians-after-muslim/

incident took place in the town of Safaga, near the Red Sea, according to the Arabic news site *El Balad*. "It's not the first time. This is happening every day," said Adel Guindy, president of Coptic Solidarity. "This one incident caught the attention of the news agencies, but there are worse things happening to the Christians every day in Egypt," he added.[103]

In another telling and very sad comment, Guindy observed, "Once the worst part of the society surfaced – the Islamists – the Copts are paying a heavy price. The West doesn't really feel our pain. It's a war of attrition."

Jason DeMars, founder of Present Truth Ministries, a Christian advocacy group that tracks religious persecution around the world, added:

> There was a relative amount of freedom (for Christians)
> before Egypt's revolution, and many were hoping for
> more freedoms, and now things are unfortunately much
> worse and much more difficult. It's what they've always
> wanted to do, but Mubarak held some of that back
> because of the support he got from the United States and
> other Western countries. People were paying attention,
> but now the extremists are seeing this as an opportunity
> to crack down on the community there.[104]

Historical Christian Community in Libya Flees

Entire books can be written about the precarious situation for Christians in Egypt. Books need to be written on the topic, given that the Coptic population there has historical importance and used to have quite large numbers, which are diminishing by the day. Some of those Christians have fled into Libya, but that move is comparable to jumping straight from frying pan to fire.

103 *http://www.humanevents.com/2013/06/03/arab-spring-egypts-legal-persecution-of-christians/* (June 7, 2013).
104 Ibid.

Just next door to Egypt, the number of Christians is far fewer, possibly resulting in the temperature toward them intensifying as numbers rise. In Libya, Christians have never been noticeably numerous, but they have lived in-country far longer than Muslims, with a church body that dates to the fourth century. The Coptic Orthodox Church predated Islam by several centuries, and until recently, numbered about 300,000. Another 140,000 Catholics once lived in Libya, along with many house churches of Muslims who have come to faith in Jesus, despite strict laws against proselytizing of Muslims by Christians.

Colonel Muammar Gaddafi talked a very loud game of Islam but did not always live it out. He accepted that Libya was overwhelmingly Islamic and did not seem to particularly care if a few historical churches continued to operate in his country, as long as they did not try to actually share their faith. This is counted as "tolerance" in Islamic countries, and when you visit these countries, you will have guides who talk on and on about how tolerant their nation is. What they are saying in essence is, "If you are from a historically Christian family, you can continue to practice that faith. We will always make you feel like an inferior, tiny minority, and don't you dare try to preach 'Jesus is Lord' outside of your church walls!" That's their idea of tolerance. I have heard this speech in Muslim countries.

A few brave Christians have lived as second-class citizens for centuries in Libya under these conditions, but after the Arab Spring, many are fleeing from there as well. Some estimates put the Christian population at only about 100,000 since the revolution. Gaddafi, like many strongman dictators, hated extremist Islamic groups, imprisoning and killing many of the leaders and members of these militias. In effect, he was protecting Christians without intentionally trying to. Now, with him removed from power, Islamists have free reign to roam and wreak havoc all over the country.

From the scattered reports that we get from Libya – many coming after the tragic deaths of four U.S. diplomatic personnel members in Benghazi on September 11, 2012 – we learn that in place of our desired vision of happy, moderate Libyans running a well-organized country after the madman was overthrown, is a very different image of a dangerous country run by militias, many of them strictly Islamic. The presence of a black flag, which is the war flag of Islam, seen anywhere, should be unsettling. An October 27, 2013 *60 Minutes* report on the Benghazi killings said such flags fly freely all over Benghazi, and other media reports relate they fly over many buildings in Tripoli as well. What that should tell us is Islamist groups, intent on "purifying" Libya, hold far more power than we have been told.

Even as I write, I am reading of an American teacher shot in Benghazi, emblematic of the purification of Libya from all "Christians."[105] The teacher was apparently a very popular one in the international school in Benghazi. Teaching at such schools has long been a way for Christians from the West to infiltrate Islamic countries and shine the light of Jesus on the next generations in those countries. You might be surprised at how freely such Christian teachers can talk about their faith in the classroom. I'm not sure if this murdered teacher talked about his love of Jesus between lectures on chemistry, but I am sure that Libya is rapidly becoming an unsafe place for Westerners, and particularly Christians of any stripe.

Here are a few documented incidents of the danger for Christians, both Libyan and foreign, in Libya today:

- An American, a South African woman, a South Korean man, and five Egyptian men were arrested in Benghazi for proselytizing. One of the Egyptians was reportedly tortured while in detention and died "of natural causes."

---

105 *http://www.foxnews.com/world/2013/12/05/american-citizen-reportedly-killed-in-benghazi/* (December 5, 2013).

The Preventive Security Section of Libya, an openly Islamist group, said it found more than forty thousand Christian books from Egypt imported by someone to Benghazi for distribution. If found guilty, all of these prisoners could face execution.[106]

- A short time after these arrests, Agence France-Presse said that Libyan authorities rounded up another fifty Egyptians for "suspect activities." These men were traders in the city market, and when busted were found to have Bibles and Christian books. Perhaps the diaspora of Egyptian Christians will one day make a huge impact on Libya, but for now, the maxim of "the blood of the martyrs is the seed of the church" appears to be coming true. Let's pray for Egyptian believers everywhere who are trying to share their faith after leaving their homeland. Their bravery is great and an example to us all.[107]

- Two Coptic Christians from Egypt were robbed and beaten, then told to repeat the Islamic confession of faith. When they refused, they were immediately shot. This type of attack occurs weekly, sources report, in the northwestern part of Libya that is essentially run by Islamist gangs.[108]

These arrests and killings make a mockery of the State Department's most recent report on religious freedom in Libya, which holds that the country's interim constitution "protects" religious freedom and that religious materials brought into the country are not censored.[109]

Even more recently, Christians in Libya have been the target

106 http://cnsnews.com/news/article/libya-imprisons-american-allegedly-prosely-tizing-christianity-benghazi (June 7, 2013).
107 Ibid.
108 http://morningstarnews.org/2013/09/two-egyptian-christians-slain-in-libya/ (December 5, 2013).
109 Ibid.

of backlash over a U.S. military action, as often occurs in Muslim countries. The targeted killing of Abu Anas al Libi in Tripoli, in October 2013, sparked a huge crackdown on any suspected Christians in the city. I have no doubt that al Libi was worthy of some sort of prosecution as an al-Qaeda operative, but the fallout of his death was the invasion of many homes and the seizing of computers and phones, and widespread arrests of anyone suspected of being a Christian.

How are these two related? When Muslims want to strike back against the U.S., they often go after the international community, and one way they can justify a crackdown on foreigners is in the name of faith. I know about this recent oppression in Tripoli thanks to an eyewitness report of a businessman who has contact with the underground Christian community there.

As I have frequently mentioned in my speaking and writing, any U.S. military action in a Muslim country usually has a disastrous impact on missionary witness in that country. This book is not intended to debate U.S. foreign policy, but you can almost – without fail – count on brutality against Christians, the church, and any missionaries in any country which the U.S. has invaded, bombed, or entered with troops. I wish there was not such a direct connection, but I can tell you as someone who ministered abroad during the U.S. invasion of Iraq in 2003, it makes life very difficult for any witness for Jesus.

My personal ministry was devastated by the invasion of Iraq, for example. Every one of my Muslim friends was angry with the U.S., and that was all they wanted to talk about with me, as the convenient representative American. Whether or not I agreed with the move was irrelevant; I was America at that point, a convenient target, and someone to scream at and threaten. Trust me, it's hard to do the work of the gospel in such an atmosphere; it's not impossible, but it's hard.

Giovanni Martinelli, the Roman Catholic archbishop of

Tripoli, summarized the Christian experience in Libya this way: "The level of security remains precarious for all foreigners, especially for Christians, because of the presence of some fundamentalist Islamic groups."[110]

The good news is that Christians from various nationalities still have a heart for Libyans and think that there are "open doors" for the spread of the gospel in that country. It is especially encouraging to read of Egyptians being arrested for having Bibles and Christian books. However, until Libya has a national army and local police forces committed to preserving the ancient Christian community there, Libyans will continue to leave the country, and those who stay will be subject to arrest and even death. In short, the Arab Spring could directly result in the end of the church in Libya, if current trends hold. As *OpenDoorsUK.org* reports: "75 percent of expat Christians have left the country ... Many Libyan Christians are fleeing their homeland. It is unlikely that the situation will change, even with a new constitution."[111]

Earliest Church Bodies in History Disperse in Syria

The situation in Syria changes so rapidly that anything written about the plight of Christians there threatens to be old news within a month. Even so, it is not difficult to paint a general picture of life for Christians and churches in this original homeland of the church, and that picture is decidedly dark. Again, the irony of U.S. foreign policy rears its ugly head as we realize that many of the Syrian rebels we either tacitly or explicitly support are chasing Christians out of the country, desecrating their buildings, and basically killing anyone who gets in the way of Allah's army.

110   www.irinnews.org/report/97653/
         security-of-christian-communities-precarious-in-libya-archbishop
111   *http://www.opendoorsuk.org/resources/worldwatch/libya.php* (December 5, 2013).

Among the millions of people who have fled Syria, a large portion of them are Christians. I doubt that I need to give you a primer on the history of Christianity in Syria. Simply remember that Paul received his vision on the road to Damascus and found salvation there. Peter himself is largely credited with being the first witness for Christ in Syria. The percentage of Syrians who worshipped in one of the many denominations there – Oriental Syriac Orthodox, Greek Orthodox, Assyrian Church of the East, Chaldean, and others – approximated the share of Christians in Egypt, about one in ten. I used the past tense of "approximate" because nearly one-half million have fled the violence as part of the wave of two million that have left the country overall.

Before the uprising in Syria, the various Christian churches were a respected part of society, with some towns and villages predominantly Christian, in fact. These bodies of believers were not bothered by the government as long as they did not upset the country's delicate social balance or speak poorly of the government. Christian meetings were monitored by secret police, but there was absolute freedom of worship.[112]

The spread of the Arab Spring to Syria, for better or worse, has radically changed the situation for Christians in this historic cradle of the faith. Plenty of photos have been distributed worldwide showing various rebels wearing priestly garb amidst Syrian church ruins, in mockery of the Christians. But the persecution has been far more serious than photo ops showing Christianity as supposedly weak, powerless, and probably finished in Syria.

As the State Department recently stated in a report on religious persecution worldwide, Syria is the chief example of the recent "largest displacement of religious communities in recent memory." In Homs, for example, the Christian community

---

112   *http://www.opendoorsuk.org/resources/worldwatch/syria.php* (December 10, 2013).

shrank from 160,000 to 1,000.[113] Eighty thousand of those
believers left in one massive migration in 2013, as NATO-backed
rebels ransacked and blew up several churches. Here's what one
Christian said about the rebels' incursion into her city:

> *They wanted to kill us because we were Christians. They*
> *were calling us 'Kaffirs,' even little children saying these*
> *things. Those who were our neighbors turned against us.*
> *At the end, when we ran away, we went through balco-*
> *nies. We did not even dare go out on the street in front*
> *of our house. I've kept in touch with the few Christian*
> *friends left back home, but I cannot speak to my Muslim*
> *friends any more. I feel very sorry about that.*[114]

Remember what I wrote earlier in this chapter about the
tenuous peace between Islamic and Christian communities.
What you will repeatedly find is that as soon
as the Islamic people in a given city or country
sense a power advantage over the Christians,
most turn on their neighbors immediately and
say and act as they have long wanted to – doing
all they can to cleanse their areas of infidels. This
is precisely what is happening in many cities in Syria.

*When Christians
hesitate to scream
"Allahu akbar!"
and take up arms,
they are quickly
slaughtered.*

Syrian Christians also face a difficult choice as Islamic rebels,
many of them openly associated with al-Qaeda, take over towns
and insist that the Christians join them or be killed. Plenty
of Syrian Christians chafe under the dictatorship of Assad,
but they also know that he has historically protected minorities. When Christians hesitate to scream "Allahu akbar!" and
take up arms, they are quickly slaughtered. One young man

---

113 http://www.christianpost.com/news/state-dept-syrian-christian-persecution-
     part-of-largest-displacement-of-religious-communities-in-recent-mem-
     ory-123987/ (August 8, 2014).
114 http://www.independent.co.uk/news/world/middle-east/the-plight-of-syrias-
     christians-we-left-homs-because-they-were-trying-to-kill-us-8274710.html
     (June 7, 2013).

from Qusayr put it this way: "They told us we must fight with them against the government. When we refused they began to threaten and insult us. They started killing Christians. Mathew Kasouha was the first they killed. He was a good man." Local Christians took up arms after a while, he said, and then there was a "showdown." More Christians were killed and he fled to Lebanon. Another young man pointed out: "It is not just the fighting and the destruction, but the division between different groups that is such a big problem. We're convinced it is the regime that's responsible for creating this, but the damage has been done. I don't know if people from different communities will ever trust each other again."[115] Prominent Christian author and educator Tony Campolo wrote recently: "It's a terrible thing to choose between participatory democracy and the freedom to live out your faith without persecution, but that's what the people of Syria are being asked to do."[116]

The sizable Armenian community in Syria has fled en masse to Lebanon and other countries. The rebels' frequent chant of "All Christians to Lebanon" seems to be coming true. Armenians are being targeted for kidnappings and killings, and many of them who are traders are losing out as rebels burn a path to Damascus, often destroying historic markets such as the one from the fourteenth century in Aleppo. One jewelry store owner put it this way in regards to Syria's future if the rebels win the war: "The history of my family is in Aleppo and we did not like leaving. Our country is being destroyed. The fact is we can only go back if Assad wins. I don't like saying this, we don't want the regime to stay as it is, but we will be safer under them."[117]

The Syrian Christians who have remained in their country,

---

115 Ibid.

116 *http://www.mennoworld.org/archived/blog/2012/1/30/
     tony-campolo-reflects-christian-persecution-middle/*

117 *http://www.independent.co.uk/news/world/middle-east/the-plight-of-syrias-
     christians-we-left-homs-because-they-were-trying-to-kill-us-8274710.html*
     (June 7, 2013).

either by stubborn choice or because they have not been able to escape yet, often remain indoors after 3:00 p.m. each day and all day on Friday, Islam's holiest day. As you might imagine, this has severely compromised these Christians' ability to make a living and even acquire the supplies they need to continue with their daily lives.[118]

Priests, bishops, nuns, and orphanage workers are being held hostage in various areas, many times being used as pawns to try to win concession from Assad's government. Christians from historically Christian-majority villages are being seized and moved to rebel-held villages that are over-whelmingly Islamist. One Christian reacted this way as she attended a prayer meeting for the twelve Orthodox Greek nuns and three orphan-age workers kidnapped: "They're coming after us. All they do is massacre people, all they know is killing." In reaction to a video released, showing the nuns speaking about being removed from the village for their safety, another prayer meeting attendee said, "They didn't even let them wear their crosses. This just shows they aren't capable of respecting Christians."[119] Does anyone in the world think these Islamist rebels have ever, or will ever, respect Christians? Imagine the fear you would feel knowing that fiery-eyed Islamists were coming to your Christian sector to take it over. If that doesn't sound like a Matthew 24 scenario, I don't know what does.

Does anyone in the world think these Islamist rebels have ever, or will ever, respect Christians?

Human Rights Watch reports that when Islamist rebels enter Christian villages in an effort to expand their territory, they seem just as intent on terrorizing Christians as they do on striking a blow to government forces. Reports include use of Christians as human shields, targeted killings of Christian

118 http://www.christianfreedom.org/the-christian-winter/persecution-in-syria/ (November 25, 2013).
119 http://www.persecution.org/2013/12/09/seizure-of-nuns-stokes-christian-fears/ (December 3, 2013).

civilians, including women and children, and widespread looting of Christians' homes and churches.[120] It is fairly obvious
that several gangs of rebels in Syria have a double agenda – win
the war, driving Assad from power, AND kill and terrorize as
many Christians as possible in doing so. Where is the outcry
over this dual scheme?

Religious leaders in the Middle East, who have excellent
access to eyewitness reports on the state of the church in Syria,
say that Christians are being targeted by rebels in an effort to
force them to migrate. One target of shells and bullets, particularly hard for believers to swallow, has been the attack
of Christian schools in Damascus and elsewhere. Patriarch
Gregorios Laham III recently said:

> These criminal acts threaten the educational process of
> our children and generations. Our diaries on missiles
> show they fall every day, especially on the neighbor-
> hoods where our parishes, churches, and institutions are
> located. This proves that this heinous war is targeting
> us and wants to terrorize our children to be prey to fear
> and frustration and migrate.[121]

In the largely Christian town of Zedad, mentioned in Ezekiel
47:15, the believers who were not able to flee the rebel incursion
were largely murdered, particularly the elderly and children.
Dozens of people, many of them quite advanced in age or stu-
dent-aged, were murdered, several by strangulation, and their
bodies were thrown into mass graves or down a well in what
has been called the worst anti-Christian act of persecution in
Syria as of this writing. In addition, fifteen hundred families
were said to be used as human shields against government

---

120 http://www.persecution.org/2013/11/21/hrw-syrian-rebel-fighters-
committed-abuses-against-civilians-and-churches-in-sadad-village/
(December 10, 2013).

121 http://www.persecution.org/2013/11/19/war-in-syria-targets-christians-says-
patriarch-laham/ (December 10, 2013).

forces during the reign of terror on the part of al-Nusra Front and Daash militias.[122]

I could write pages and pages about individual attacks on our fellow believers in Jesus as a result of the Islamist rebel influx into Syria, but you can explore the many websites that deal with this matter. To take a more general view of what is happening in Syria, I like the headline of a recent article in *The Spectator,* an online newspaper: "Whoever wins in Syria, its Christians will lose."[123] Robin Harris summarizes this well for his column:

> *Large areas of opposition-held Syria are now under sharia law. Saudi judges have appeared to administer it. Non-Muslims are only tolerated if they pay the jizya, the tax imposed on infidels. Priests are special targets. This is where a Syrian Catholic priest, Father François Murad, was murdered last month. He was not the first to die. A Syrian Orthodox priest, Father Fadi Haddad, was grabbed last December as he left his church to negotiate the release of a kidnapped parishioner. His body was found by the roadside, the eyes gouged out. Two higher-profile recent cases – if not high enough for the government or most of our press to notice – are those of the Greek Orthodox archbishop Paul Yazigi and the Syriac Orthodox archbishop Yohanna Ibrahim. They were seized near Aleppo in April, when trying to negotiate the release of kidnapped priests. Both archbishops are now presumed dead.*[124]

On the roads that lead to Damascus, where Paul once trod and Peter journeyed to share the good news he was so excited

---

122 *http://www.persecution.org/2013/11/12/reports-of-torture-from-christian-survivors-in-syria/* (December 10, 2013).

123 *http://www.spectator.co.uk/features/9006591/dont-expect-the-government-to-raise-its-voice-for-syrias-christians/* (December 10, 2013).

124 Ibid.

about, waves of Islamist rebels from a variety of countries are doing all they can to not only overthrow Assad, but to also either kill or make so uncomfortable the hundreds of thousands of Christians, that Syria will become a bona fide Islamic republic. I will share in chapter 6 about the brave believers who have elected to stay in their homeland and show God's love to their enemies. But remember as you watch the evening news that your very brothers and sisters are being tortured and killed, their schools and businesses are bombed and burned, and their churches desecrated, even if that does not make it to your nightly newscast.

Christians in Tunisia Fear Persecution

Fewer dramatic stories of strangulations and the bodies of entire families being thrown down wells can be told from Tunisia, thank God, but make no mistake that Christians there are feeling the heat and waiting nervously for the new government to chart its course and refine the country's constitution.

As I mentioned in chapter 2, Tunisia has a long history of feeling almost European, of tolerating different interpretations of Islam, and of encouraging education for both boys and girls. What tiny Christian community that has remained there over the centuries has not had any significant worries – until the Arab Spring. Tunisia was 99 percent or more Islamic before the Arab Spring, so it's not a country where you will read daily stories about Christians being driven from their homelands or churches being burned. In fact, there are only a small handful of churches in the entire country, most of them Roman Catholic, and Muslims outnumber Christians twenty-five thousand to one.[125]

The Christian community is comprised largely of Tunisians

---

125 *http://www.christianfreedom.org/the-christian-winter/persecution-in-tunisia/* (December 10, 2013).

of Italian and French descent, and a group of Berber Arab believers, all of whom combined form a group of a mere twenty-five thousand people scattered throughout the country. Twenty thousand of these Christians are Catholic, who worship in a dozen churches and operate nine schools, several libraries, clinics, and a monastery. Protestants number about two thousand, with a Muslim Background Believer community of a few hundred.

When the Arab Spring was launched in Tunisia, believers there had hoped it would liberalize the country's laws, which were deceptively repressive, including a ban on proselytization and the importation of Christian literature in Arabic. Instead, those hopes have been dashed as Salafists and other conservative groups have stepped into the power vacuum and increased its sometimes-violent activities. In addition to fear about a new Islamist constitution in Tunisia, Christian groups have reported an upsurge in government surveillance of their activities, both expatriate churches and indigenous ones.[126]

The draft constitution names *sharia* law as the "principal source of legislation"; thus, one can only hazard a guess regarding the future state of the tiny, weak church in Tunisia.[127] The best-case scenario would be liberals in the country's political establishment being able to stave off *sharia* as the law of the land. However, if Tunisia does become like Libya, and other Arab Spring countries will also, with Islamists firmly in power, we can only hope that Muslims will be drawn to Jesus through the brave witness of Christians who refuse to yield to harassment, beatings, and worse after converting from Islam. The homeland of early church giants Tertullian and Cyprian will continue to debate just how far right it will move as Salafists and other groups seek to exercise influence during government debates over what kind of society Tunisia will create.

---

126 Ibid.
127 *http://barnabasfund.org/UK/Tunisia.html* (December 10, 2013).

A Summary of the Plight of Christians
in the Countries of the Arab Spring

Christians have lived for centuries in the countries of the Arab Spring. They have often risen to high levels of society, despite being despised by many Muslims and discriminated against in many ways. They have grown just as tired of corruption and dictatorship as Muslims have, but they realized long ago that the strongman in place ensured that Islamist ideas and gangs would be held in check, sometimes even put in prison. The always tenuous détente between Muslims and Christians in these countries rested on the authority of the dictators there.

When the Arab Spring erupted, Christians were happy to speculate on what a truly free country would look like. Would they have new freedoms to share their faith, import Christian literature, and build new churches? The prospect of emerging from under the fist of a dictator appealed to many believers, who hoped to have a greater role in society and play a part in establishing democracies with novel concepts such as true freedom of religion and speech.

However, many other Christians were wary from the beginning. They knew that once the authoritarian leader was swept aside, society's more lawless elements would emerge in the power vacuum. They also had enough familiarity with the hard, cold, merciless face of Islam to know that once a more "pure" Islam came to their societies and halls of power, Christians would need to leave or would be oppressed in a new way. Those prophetic Christians were correct. In Libya, Egypt, Tunisia, and now Syria, Christians are seen as unclean elements in society and a people group to be driven out, killed, or systematically subjugated. Muslims have done this throughout their history in the Middle East by imposing taxes on infidels, disallowing construction of new worship facilities, and limiting public worship.

Fortunately, some voices from both the Christian and secular world have started to emerge to draw attention to this budding genocide. Ayaan Hirsi Ali, a visiting fellow at the American Enterprise Institute and a self-proclaimed atheist who grew up in Somalia, has written several books critical of Islam, all of which you should read. She recently penned a *Newsweek* article titled "The Global War on Christians in the Muslim World," in which she stated that "Christians are being killed in the Islamic world because of their religion. It is a rising genocide that ought to provoke global alarm."

She reported that in recent years:

> *The violent oppression of Christian minorities has become the norm in Muslim-majority nations stretching from West Africa and the Middle East to South Asia and Oceania. The conspiracy of silence surrounding this violent expression of religious intolerance has to stop. Nothing less than the fate of Christianity – and ultimately of all religious minorities – in the Islamic world is at stake.*[128]

Ms. Hirsi Ali, who has a lifetime of experience with the more intolerant and brutal side of Islam, is right again. Who is behind this "conspiracy of silence" that she mentions? That would be the topic for an entire other book, but let's put at least part of the blame on the new philosophical norms that hold to the idea of all truths being equal, thus all faiths must be respected and never criticized or evaluated on a moral basis. Hirsi Ali is also correct in stating that the world's reaction to the fate of Christians in the Middle East will determine if our faith will continue to exist in that region of the world. I am guessing it will not, judging from the scant reports on the problem and the political momentum of Islamists in the countries of the Arab Spring.

---

128   *http://www.newsweek.com/ayaan-hirsi-alithe-global-war-christians-muslim-world-65817* (December 10, 2013).

Christian author and professor emeritus of sociology at Eastern University (among several other titles) Tony Campolo, not known for his conservative stance on anything to do with politics or policy, raised his voice a bit when writing recently about the plight of believers in the Middle East. His comments deserve a wide reading and are indicative of American optimism about the Arab Spring that has turned into a very disappointing realism:

> *Many claim that what was happening in countries like Tunisia, Libya, and Egypt represented the emergence of participatory democracy. Those of us who were political activists during the 60s believed that the call 'All power to the people!' was being heeded. The problem was that we never asked who the people were and what the people wanted. Over and over again, in each of the revolutions in Northern Africa, we were told that the moderate Muslims would win out and create fair and just rule for all people, but in each and every case, we have witnessed the emergence of the Muslim Brotherhood who are well organized and able to usurp power. This extremist group has no patience or tolerance for Christians.*

Campolo, as is his wont, identifies precisely the question that few observers asked as the Arab Spring sprung. No one dug deep enough to find out "who the people were and what the people wanted." Those of us who have lived in Islamic communities and had some awareness of what was occurring on the streets in those countries, due to friends in those places and general knowledge of pure Islam, had a feeling that the will of the people would be unleashed, and that it would be a very conservative Islamic will.

In a day of political correctness, what is wrong with people who value religion highly and take over a government? That's

WHAT THE ARAB SPRING MEANS FOR CHRISTIANS

pretty much what a lot of evangelical Christians long for in the U.S., right? Campolo identifies the danger:

> We are inclined to believe that democracy is when the majority rules and free elections take place wherein every citizen has the right to vote. That, indeed, is a very superficial definition of democracy. At least we should add to that statement that democracy requires a political system wherein it is safe to be in the minority.

Bingo! There is the problem in Islamist "democracies" created as a result of the Arab Spring. Campolo later called all of us to action, as I hope this book does, as he encouraged a hard look at the consequences of the Arab Spring:

> These are difficult days. It's easy to get swept away by the populace without asking some severe questions about religious freedom. In the Arab Spring, there doesn't seem to be much freedom of religion emerging, and we had better stand up, take notice, and do something to stop the tendencies towards religious persecution that we are beginning to see evident in those places.[129]

Ghaffar Hussain, a counterterrorism expert in Great Britain, added his voice of concern with how the religious, political, and ethnic landscape has changed in the Middle East as a result of the Arab Spring. As he succinctly put it:

> The world is increasingly realizing that the Arab Spring also has a dark under-belly. As well as ushering in nascent and fragile democracies, popular uprisings in the MENA (Middle East, Europe, North Africa) region have unleashed previously suppressed reactionary forces. This has resulted in more jihadist intimidation, sectarian strife, and political in-fighting. It has

---

129 http://www.redletterchristians.org/reflections-on-the-arab-spring-and-the-persecution-of-christians/ (June 7, 2013).

also resulted in the systematic persecution of one of the region's oldest minority communities.[130]

Why hasn't more been done to protect followers of Jesus in the Arab Spring countries? Ghaffar has a fascinating slant, which I believe is right on the money:

> *The persecution of Arab Christians is a phenomenon that no one wants to prioritize. It just doesn't fit neatly into anyone's political narrative. As the outside world focuses on the movements of al-Qaeda-linked groups and the jostling for executive political power between Islamists, nationalists, and liberals, the plight of the Middle East's Christians will continue to be ignored.*[131]

I wish he were wrong, but I fear he is right. Christians are criminally overlooked as political narratives are shaped. The end result is millions living as refugees in foreign lands, or not going out of their homes after dark or on Fridays.

This silence has spawned some fascinating conspiracy theories, which are never in short supply in the developing world. I had many conversations with educated Turks who believed that September 11 was an American plot, with sophisticated French people who were sure that the U.S. was hiding Osama bin Laden to continue its incursion in the Middle East, and with African neighbors who claimed that the Y2K scare was a hoax perpetrated by Americans to force the world to look to the U.S. for (costly) solutions in anticipation of a global computer crash. (Well, in one out of three theories, the developing world was correct!)

Anyway, one idea that is gaining steam in the Middle East is that somehow the United States and Israel are behind the muteness surrounding the cleansing of Arab Spring countries

---

130 http://www.thecommentator.com/article/2251/christians_the_forgotten_victims_of_the_arab_spring (June 7, 2013).
131 Ibid.

of Christians and their influence. Issam John Darwish, the archbishop of several towns in Syria, put it this way:

> I think the situation is being manipulated by the USA and maybe Israel – they want this to happen. I have raised this with officials in the West; they must bring peace. The jihadis will not stop here, the war will spread to Europe. What will England be like in 10 or 15 years?[132]

While I do not believe for a millisecond that there is any conspiracy behind the feeble reaction to the persecution of Christians in Arab Spring countries, you can imagine the befuddlement of believers in the Middle East accustomed to strong U.S. military actions when a people group is threatened with extermination. "Where are the troops?" our brothers and sisters in the faith ask.

Whether or not we agree with the archbishop's claim that the U.S. has ultimately been "behind" the rise of Islamism's iron fist in Middle Eastern countries since 2011, we should pay heed to his warning that jihadis gain strength like a snowball rolling down a hill. His question about England is a good one indeed.

I'll close this chapter with one simple sentence that I believe sums up well what has occurred in the countries of the Arab Spring. Contrasting earlier persecution of Christians who faced trouble when sharing their faith during the expansion of the kingdom in the first centuries after Christ with what is happening now, Robin Harris concluded his outstanding column on the fate of Christians in the Middle East with: "The story is not of expansion accompanied by persecution but of persecution leading to elimination."[133]

Did you read that last word? "Elimination." Our brothers

132   http://www.catholic.org/international/international_story.php?id=51428 (November 11, 2013).

133   http://www.spectator.co.uk/features/9006591/ dont-expect-the-government-to-raise-its-voice-for-syrias-christians/.

and sisters in the Middle East are living Matthew 24 right now. Could this type of living in fear due to Islamic fundamentalism spread to our dear shores? I absolutely believe it can. In order for that to happen, though, the Islamic world would have to gain a lot of strength to challenge the West for global supremacy. To become a true bloc of nations, Muslim countries would have to unite in a way that they have not for one hundred and fifty years. What kind of conditions could create a unified, powerful coalition of countries under the banner of Islam? What events could precipitate a union of Sunni and Shiite, Iran and Saudi Arabia? I have a few ideas.

CHAPTER FOUR

How the World Will Sway Towards Islam

Right now, as 2014 stumbles to its completion, I can understand how you might not be able to envision a world where Islam rules the nations as a caliph calls the shots as a one-world leader. This scenario is the stuff of fantasy – unless you believe that biblical prophecy could be fulfilled within the next couple of decades, and that there *will* be a solitary leader who has control of the world's armies – a coming reality that even barely informed Christians agree on, no matter what particular interpretation of prophecy they favor.

Will that fearsome world leader, known as the Antichrist, be a Muslim? I think it's probable, based on the clues that I spelled out in my first book and all that has occurred since its publication in 2005. Not a single world event has occurred that would nullify the thesis laid out in that book. In fact, several developments have sped history in the direction that I and others foresee, as chronicled in earlier chapters. Yet, if a Muslim Antichrist is going to rule the entire world, he must first rule a united *Islamic* world. That bloc of countries, and its people, must have the power and leverage to challenge the West. A united Islamic *ummah* might seem as much of a pipe dream as an Islamic Antichrist. Today, Islam's divisions are on plain display in Syria. Secularist Baathists still run the country (as of this writing); Sunni Islamists comprise the bulk of the rebels who have captured a sizeable swath of the country; and Sunni moderates plead for foreign assistance to seize power in the rebel "coalition," all while Shiite Iran and Hezbollah battle the rebels to prop up embattled Prime Minister al-Assad to block a wider Sunni influence in the Middle East.

Muslims are not unaware of their lack of unity, and I believe the idea is growing among them that unless they do unite, they will never be able to challenge the secular West for supremacy over world affairs. Away from the glare of Western television news cameras, Muslims hold rallies where they call for a united Islam under a new caliph, a superman who will spearhead the "liberation of Palestine from the hated Jews" and the "freeing of mankind from the chains of capitalism."[134] Whether or not this caliph is someone we think about or look for, he is definitely on the radar screen of Muslims worldwide who long to see Islam become the greatest force for good (and Allah) on our planet.

As the fallout from the Arab Spring continues and Islamists gain more political power than almost any Western observer predicted, it seems as if the world is hardening into factions – "Islam is the answer" versus "Tolerance for all and freedom of conscience." This theory of Harvard political scientist Samuel Huntington in his book *The Clash of Civilizations and Remaking of the World Order*, so ridiculed after it debuted in 1996, now seems poignant as terrorists threaten the Olympic Games, Western nations tighten immigration laws, and tens of millions of Muslims vote that the Koran should indeed be the constitution of their countries. Islamists now hold the reins in several Arab Spring countries, and another breed of Islamists re-take more of Iraq and Afghanistan every day. As noted Christian speaker Tony Campolo recently wrote on his blog:

> Huntington … predicted that sometime in the 21st century there could arise a war between the Islamic nations and the western world. Many scoff at this, but more and

---

134 http://www.israelnationalnews.com/News/News.aspx/168639 (December 19, 2013).

more I have come to believe that it could happen, especially as radicals in the Islamic community gain control of governments. History is often controlled by disciplined minorities.[135]

Yet, what is the "Islamic community," as the centuries-old, often violent, division between Sunni and Shiite persists? People ask, "How will the Sunnis and Shiites lay aside their differences, which have produced several wars and constant skirmishes in the past few decades?" This is the question I receive most when I speak about a coming Islamic bloc governed by a new caliph. It is a fair and valid question, and it is difficult to answer. In responding to that query, I lean most heavily on a scenario where the Islamic world is attacked severely enough by Western countries, or Israel, that Muslims will band together in the spirit of the Arab proverb: "The enemy of my enemy is my friend."

I won't spend pages explaining the differences between Sunni and Shiite; all you need to know for this chapter is that Shiites believe that the caliphate should have remained in Muhammad's bloodline, and they resent to this day the assassination of Muhammad's grandson Hussein. The Sunni-Shiite split is largely political, and the two branches have slightly different practices and beliefs, although it should be stated that almost half of Sunnis view Shiites as impure Muslims for various reasons.[136]

What can erase this divide? What would the Islamic world look like if it were fused together by a common threat? I have chosen three possible contexts (among myriad possibilities) that could produce a Muslim bloc of countries standing toe to toe with the West, laying out terms that the West must abide

---

135 *http://www.redletterchristians.org/*
      reflections-on-the-arab-spring-and-the-persecution-of-christians/.
136 *http://www.economist.com/blogs/economist-explains/2013/05/economist-*
      explains-19 (December 27, 2013). This is one of many places to find a brief
      summary of this split.

by if it wants peace. I will tackle these hypothetical situations in order of likelihood and immediacy:

- Israel bombs Iran and the Islamic world unites in defense of its persecuted brothers.

- Fundamentalists seize access to nuclear weapons, probably in Pakistan.

- Islamists seize control of the oil reserves in Saudi Arabia and other nations.

Will Israel Bomb Iran?

As I write in the summer of 2014, this question continues to hang in the air, especially after U.S. negotiations with Iran have led to a six-month suspension of that country's nuclear program. The particulars are still being hammered out, and no one is really sure if Iran will abide by the agreement and halt its progress toward making a nuclear bomb.[137] There has been widespread criticism of this deal, as cynics doubt the integrity of Iran and remain convinced that the country will produce nuclear weapons someday, no matter what sanctions are pinned on it. I would tend to agree with this viewpoint. If I had to guess, I would say that Iran will stall the West enough during these current negotiations and subsequent "inspections" to achieve its end. What happens as this process slogs along will be most intriguing to watch. Will Israel, tired of a lack of will in the West, bomb Iran? Will the U.S. attack Iran in some way other than at press conferences or via economic sanctions?

Let's spend a few pages looking at the case for Israel bombing Iran, a possibility that has loomed since 1991, according to Kenneth Pollack, a highly regarded Middle East policy expert

---

137 *http://www.latimes.com/world/la-fg-iran-deal-20131218,0,7670834. story#axzz2oJSTKvhG* (December 23, 2013).

at the Brookings Institution in Washington.[138] Pollack, who has written an entire book on this issue, clarifies the possibility of Israel bombing Iran in expert fashion, arguing for caution before anyone assumes that Israel will proceed with this mission.

Pollack's primary argument *against* Israel bombing Iran rests on four paradoxes that he describes in detail:

- It will spur Iran to rebuild, and probably to weaponize anyway.

- It will undermine the inspections and sanctions needed to prevent Iran from rebuilding.

- It requires American support, but could alienate the United States.

- It will provoke that which it is meant to prevent.[139]

Regarding his first point, Pollack notes: "There are few events that would be more likely to convince Tehran to rebuild its program (and even acquire an outright nuclear arsenal) than an Israeli attack."[140] I certainly agree with Pollack here.

As for point 2, Pollack says, "an Israeli strike would be the surest way to undermine the diplomatic foundations of sanctions and inspections."[141] Would that be a huge loss? Yes, to those who have done the hard work of diplomacy, and no, to those who believe the sanctions and inspections have not deterred Iran's progress towards joining the nuclear club.

To fill out point 3, Pollack says that Washington would be infuriated with an Israeli strike and would be especially peeved about the possibility of Iranian retaliation against the

---

138 Kenneth Pollack, *Unthinkable: Iran, the Bomb, and American Strategy* (New York, NY: Simon and Schuster, 2013), 183.

139 Ibid., 185.

140 Ibid.

141 Ibid.

U.S.[142] Will Israel ultimately care what Washington thinks? It has not always.

Pollack's logic might reach its apex with point 4 as he says, "an Israeli air strike on the Iranian nuclear program would almost certainly provoke Iran and its allies to attack Israel."[143] Again, I'm not sure if Israel lives in fear of future attack, although I agree with Pollack and believe that an air strike would provoke a prolonged response from Iran and Hezbollah.

Pollack further builds his case against an Israeli air strike by detailing the difficulty of such a mission: the distance to be traveled, the problem of eluding radar on the return trip, and the challenge of destroying Iran's nuclear labs, one of which is located below more than a football field-size area of solid rock. The effectiveness of bombs on the Fordow enrichment facility, a prime target, is questionable, at best.[144]

Pollack adds to his argument against an Israeli air strike by raising the possibility that Iran has secret nuclear sites that no one outside of that secretive country even knows about, another very real prospect. Pollack's final argument centers on how long the most fearsome Israeli air strike could delay Iran's assembly of a nuclear weapon: most expert observers predict, at most, a one- to two-year slowdown of that process, *not* an abandonment of that goal.[145]

Despite all of these potential impediments, Pollack admits:

> *Israeli skill, creativity, and technical competence are high enough that we should not assume that they can't pull it off. If anyone can, it is the Israeli Defense Force. But neither should we assume that it would be easy. It*

---

142 Ibid.
143 Ibid., 186.
144 Ibid., 192.
145 Ibid., 195-199.

sure won't be. It isn't that Israel can't do it, just that it would be very hard to succeed and very easy to fail.[146]

I don't pretend to have the technical expertise that Pollack has, but I do know that Israel has twice annihilated nuclear reactors in neighboring countries – in Iraq in 1981 and in Syria in 2007. I think that Israel will grow tired of seeing Western negotiators continually outflanked by Iranian representatives, who I believe will delay inspection of their nuclear facilities while continuing to advance in their mission to create nuclear weapons.

> *I think that Israel will grow tired of seeing Western negotiators continually outflanked by Iranian representatives.*

Prime Minister Benjamin Netanyahu, during one recent visit to the U.S., has gone on public record as saying that "My priority ... for a next term as prime minister, will be first to stop Iran from getting nuclear weapons."[147] Why does he feel so strongly about this? Because he has an insight into Islamic thought that many Westerners do not. As Pollack reports:

> *He [Netanyahu] reportedly believes that the United States does not understand Iran and its leadership, at least as he believes they should be understood, saying of the American government, 'They know it's [Iran with a nuclear weapons capability] is a very bad thing, but they need to understand the convulsive power of militant Islam ... the cult of death, the ideological zeal.'*[148]

There's a man who understands Islamism!

If and when Israel does bomb Iran, I think we will see the first step towards a far more united Islamic world, as the despised Zionists boldly invade Muslim territory. Pollack notes that an air strike *could rally at least some portion of the Arab and Islamic worlds to Iran's defense (even if only diplomatically and*

146 Ibid., 194-195.
147 Ibid., 215.
148 Ibid.

rhetorically) because Iran will have been attacked by the hated Israelis. Even those Muslim countries that hate the Iranians would find it hard to criticize Iran, let alone take action against it.[149]

Add to that a strong international reaction against Israel, and you have a scenario that Muslims dream about: Iran as victim, Muslims as martyrs, and Israel as the immoral bully. Which side would France, for example, take as Hezbollah rockets rain down on Israel in response? Where would Russia fall? China? Suddenly, we would be one giant step closer to all nations being against Israel, a central theme of End Times prophecy. Even the U.S. would have leaders saying privately, "Let Israel deal with these attacks; it deserves them."

What would a more united Islam look like after an Israeli attack? Israel's oldest newspaper, *Haaretz,* offers a few ideas, inviting guest columnist Ahmed Rashid from Pakistan to outline the probable Islamic response to a bombing of Iran. In a recent column, Rashid noted:

- Iran has already "trained local militants to attack U.S. targets" in countries that have sizeable Shiite populations, from Lebanon to India, including Pakistan, Afghanistan, Bahrain, and Iraq. During George W. Bush's second term, "Iran organized and planned for retaliatory attacks against U.S. targets everywhere that it was in a position to arm and fund clandestine groups."

- "The Shia protest in the Muslim world would likely be organized and widespread, and would target Americans and Israelis, and include major acts of terrorism and extreme violence."

- In Sunni countries such as Pakistan and Afghanistan, where anti-American feelings already run high, "Any attack on Iran could see a merging of all these Sunni

---

149   Ibid., 208.

elements as well as of the broader Sunni population, and one could expect widespread anger in the streets."

- These protests "could make it almost impossible for Americans or Israelis to travel, work or do business across the Arab world and the Indian subcontinent."

- The protests could also "lead to a reinforcing of Islamic fundamentalist parties" in Arab Spring countries, "which could be expected to jump on the anti-American bandwagon."

- Other consequences could include a strengthening of the Taliban in Afghanistan and a "possible new intifada among the Palestinians."

Rashid's summary statements sound ominous:

Thus any attack on Iran can be expected to unleash a violent reaction throughout the Muslim world, both in the more organized Shia minority camp where Iran has influence and in the majority Sunni countries where Iran may not have influence, but anti-Americanism certainly does. The United States will find itself besieged in many parts of the Muslim world, making normal diplomacy unworkable and the effort to enlist Muslim states to support the U.S. war against Al-Qaida more difficult.[150]

Before you read on, re-read the bullet points above and think about what this new world would look like. As someone who loves to travel and live abroad, I am particularly struck by Rashid's point about travel in the Arab world becoming "impossible" for Americans. If Israel does bomb Iran, we could have a much more segmented, tribal world, where people of certain countries would not dare to venture into specific foreign regions.

---

150 *http://www.haaretz.com/opinion/what-an-israeli-attack-on-iran-will-mean-for-the-muslims-1.429646* (December 27, 2013).

That's a real loss to the world and its citizens, as well as another strike against the peaceful globalization that some thought the Internet, Microsoft, and Apple could produce. This is why I tell people who are considering a ministry to the Islamic world to *go now*, while the window is still partially open. After an Israeli attack on Iran, I think the window will be slammed shut.

I also think Rashid makes an excellent point about Islamism in Arab Spring countries. All of the rhetoric about the U.S. and Israel secretly wanting to wipe Islam off the planet will ring true if Israel bombs Iran. The swing in Arab Spring countries that I described in my first several chapters will gain even more momentum, post-attack.

Of course, the state of affairs described above is just one man's opinion, but I think we should pay particular attention to the opinions of Muslims within Islamic countries, such as Rashid, who have a better pulse on the Islamic world than we do. I don't want to sound like Chicken Little, but I've spent enough time around Muslims to get a sense for their hatred of Israel and their willingness to unite if they can point to a concerted Israeli attempt to resume an active "war" against Muslim countries. I also think that we are moving inexorably towards a global separation along religious and cultural lines, and the Israeli bombing of Iran will only accelerate this movement.

As central authority has diminished both on a national and international level in many parts of the world, particularly in countries of the Arab Spring, religion has often filled the power vacuum. In short, "Islam is the answer" sounds much more appealing when there is no central government acting in the best interests of its citizens, as is the case in Syria and Libya now. As central governments' authority weakens and religion gains strength, conditions favorable for a global caliphate of Muslims emerge. Robert Kaplan, the chief geopolitical analyst for Stratfor, a global intelligence firm, and a widely traveled author and writer, summed up where our world is moving in a recent article for *Foreign Policy* magazine. His conclusion merits consideration, as he compares our current decade with the period entitled "Late Antiquity" after the fall of the Roman Empire:

> In *The* City of God, *St. Augustine revealed that it is the devout – those in search of grace – who have no reason to fear the future. And as the tribes of old now slowly come undone in the unstoppable meat grinder of developing-world urbanization, religion will be more necessary than ever as a replacement. Alas, extremist Islam (as well as evangelical Christianity and Orthodox Judaism in the West) may make perfect sense for our age, even as its nemesis may not be democracy but new forms of military authority. Late Antiquity is useful to the degree that it makes us humble about what awaits us. But whatever comes next, the charmed circle of Western elites is decidedly not in control.*[151]

In essence, I believe a bombing of Iran will draw clear battle lines that most Muslims already assume exist: the U.S. and Israel versus the Islamic world. Where does Europe come in? I am betting that most, if not all, European countries would loudly condemn Israel for its aggressive act and state (again) that negotiations are always preferable to war.

Marvin Weinbaum, the director of the Middle East Institute's Center for Pakistan Studies, and a former intelligence analyst for Pakistan and Afghanistan in the State Department, agrees with Rashid, predicting that "the ramifications of an Israeli strike on Iran could extend beyond the region."[152] Weinbaum believes that some of those ramifications would include a blockage of NATO supply routes to Afghanistan, possible cancellation of

---

151 http://www.foreignpolicy.com/articles/2013/12/03/augustine_s_world_what_
antiquity_tells_us_about_syria (January 7, 2014).

152 http://nationalinterest.org/commentary/what-iran-attack-means-afpak-
7519?page=1 (December 27, 2013).

air rights over Pakistan, and a subsequent aid cutoff and rupture of relations between our country and Pakistan, allowing a "strengthened jihadi narrative" there.[153]

In summary, Israel bombing Iran will awaken the Muslim world to a long-time enemy and unite Muslims against Israel and the "Zionist" U.S. It will create a perfect Petri dish for Islamism to thrive, as Muslims construct a compelling narrative that Israel and the U.S. do indeed want to wipe Islam from the face of the earth. As that message is spread around the world, it will not matter to Muslims if they are Shiite in Lebanon or Sunni in Turkey. They will amalgamate to defend what they have in common. This temporary unity will dissolve quickly unless someone can bridge the Sunni-Shiite gap and maintain the momentum toward a unified Muslim world, a caliphate. I will portray the type of leader needed later in this chapter.

How Fundamentalists Could Seize Access to Nuclear Weapons

The first step in this chapter about the unification of Muslims has a closer relationship with the second step than you might realize. If Pakistan's quite sizable Islamist segment of the population is aroused by an attack on Islam, it will put more pressure than ever on its government to back away from cooperation with the U.S. Many analysts, including Weinbaum, think that as this occurs, the U.S. will have a much more difficult time tracking the growth and development of terrorist organizations in Pakistan.[154]

How Islamist is Pakistan? It's difficult to grade the influence of Islamism in Pakistan, but we should not forget that Islamists were part of Pakistan's core constituency from the time the country was born in 1949, and both the government and the

---

153 Ibid.
154 Ibid.

military have open Islamists in their leadership ranks today. Here are a few words from Pakistan's "Objectives Resolution" in its first Constituent Assembly, which sound very different than the original secular visions of places such as Turkey and Tunisia: "The purpose of the state is to enable Muslims 'to order their lives in the individual and collective spheres in accordance with the teachings and requirements of Islam as set out in the Holy Quran and the Sunna.'"[155]

Pakistan has long acted as a facilitator of Islamic unity, hosting Muslim Brotherhood conferences for decades and designating Karachi as the capital of the World Muslim Congress. Tens of thousands of jihadists who fought the Soviets in Afghanistan came from Pakistan and returned there after their victory, and of course, we all know that Pakistan allowed Osama bin Laden to live safely within its borders for years. Don't picture Pakistan as a secularized country with a few rural regions controlled by a couple of pesky Islamist militias. Rather, see it as a country that considers itself a leader in the Islamic world, crucial to protecting Islam's purity and influence worldwide, a country where Islamist politicians control massive districts.

The deeper you dig into Pakistan, the more influence you will see Islamism having.

The deeper you dig into Pakistan, the more influence you will see Islamism having. This truth has particular interest to me because my previous writings have attracted stern criticism from former missionaries to Muslims, embodied most forcefully by Warren Larson's stinging appraisal of my first book in *Christianity Today*.[156] Other critiques of my book condemn my negative assumptions of the worst about the Islamic world. Those criticisms do not hurt my feelings; differences of opinion make the world go around. I am intrigued, however, by what

155 *http://www.currenttrends.org/research/detail/islamism-and-the-pakistani-state* (January 9, 2014).
156 *http://www.ctlibrary.com/ct/2006/june/29.38.html* (January 16, 2014).

many of these critics have in common: they served in Pakistan decades ago, when that country had far less Islamist influence and at least tried to appear to be a secularized democracy. I tell all of those critics, whom I respect, that the world has changed a lot since 1970, particularly Pakistan. This is not your father's Islam, in Pakistan or anywhere else.

Husain Haqqani, the former ambassador from Pakistan to the U.S., and a current professor at Boston University, divides Islamists in Pakistan into three categories: 1) those that work within the government; 2) those that want to win places of power in the government; and 3) those that want to take over the government through force. One of his recent articles describes a political group that sees "jihad as a sacred right and obligation" and has trained many of the al-Qaeda groups in Afghanistan. That group, called JUI for short, also wants to see Pakistan become an Islamic state.[157]

Other Islamist groups are not only acknowledged by the Pakistani government, but are also allowed to operate openly, being vigorously anti-Israel and anti-American. They see the battle for world power in religious terms and call their followers to sacrifice. One of these parties' leaders said this in a recent speech:

> The Muslim Ummah is in a big problem right now with India, Israel and America using all their technological advancements against us and they are attacking Pakistan. The Muslim Ummah needs to reduce all the conspiracies of the disbelievers to dust. The problems in Burma, Kashmir, Palestine, and Afghanistan can only be resolved by making sacrifices in the battlefield.[158]

That same leader, Hafiz Muhammad Saeed, has had a

---

157 Ibid.
158 http://judofficial.wordpress.com/2013/07/06/hafiz-saeeds-advice-for-pakistan-to-emerge-as-a-leader-of-the-muslim-umma (January 9, 2014).

ten-million-dollar price put on his head by the U.S., urging his prosecution. Yet he runs his organization, the Army of the Pure, in open sight in Pakistan, inciting his countrymen with quotes like this: "Wage jihad against America in order to save Pakistan and Islam."[159]

Another group, Islamic Society, states clearly that its objective is "a Divine Government" that prompts "universal revolution in the individual and collective life of man that Islam calls for." Please note the word "universal" and understand that Islamist groups do not look merely to the borders of their respective countries when they think about Islamic revolution. The group states that it will not achieve this revolution via underground means, but "will do everything openly" as it seeks to win power in Pakistan's government. Backed by Saudi dollars, it aims to greatly increase its share of seats in Parliament.[160]

Islamic Society is not shy about its anti-American stance, saying that as it gains power, it will increase the stature of Pakistan and end "U.S. slavery, to restore Pakistan's independence and sovereignty," all part of re-establishing a society modeled after the prophet Muhammad's governing in Medina nearly fourteen hundred years ago.[161] The party looks to form alliances with other, more popular groups to increase its impact, even if it can't win a majority in Parliament. This type of party collaboration is common in most elected governments outside of the U.S. Perhaps that is why Pakistan's Movement for Justice, led by world-famous cricketer Imran Kahn, one of the final two candidates for Pakistan's prime minister position in 2013, sounded more Islamic than Western in campaign pronouncements. Khan had several choice sound bites, from "Sharia is

---

159   "Hafiz Saeed calls for Jihad Against America," *AFP*, April 6, 2012 (January 9, 2014).

160   Jamaat-e-Islami Pakistan website, *http://jamaat.org/beta/site/page/4* (January 9, 2014).

161   Jamaat slogan & election manifesto for 2013 elections, *http://election2013. geo.tv/parties/detail/32/ jamaateislamipakistan.html* (January 9, 2014).

what makes us human" to "Sharia is what brings justice and humanity in society."[162]

The final type of movement, which seeks to work outside the political realm, is called the Party of Islamic Liberation, and is legally banned in the country. This party sees Pakistan as the springboard for restoring the caliphate, stating, "The Islamic countries are Muslim Lands that were divided by the agents of Kafir (infidel) colonialists, as part of their plan to abolish the Khilafah. According to Sharia unifying them into one state is obligatory."[163] You can't find a much clearer vision than that on the Web!

This party has had members arrested as they seek to infiltrate the army, assassinate political leaders, and stage a coup in an attempt to turn Pakistan completely Islamist as a way to usher in Allah's kingdom on earth.[164] You need to know that these goals are shared by millions of Pakistanis, with dozens of senior leaders working day and night, with patience, to see them fulfilled. Combine this Islamist perspective with nuclear capability and I think you know where it could lead.

Anti-American and Israel sentiment is not an exclusively rural mindset in Pakistan, nor is it a secret one. It is part of the national discourse, makes daily headlines, and evinces the continuing struggle for the soul of a nuclear country. Hussain summarizes it well:

> *Pakistan's national discourse encourages Islamists to wield influence disproportionate to their numbers. It also allows militant groups to organize, recruit, train and*

---

162 Imran Khan's press conference in Peshawar, October 11, 2012, *http://www. youtube.com/watch?v= l3waV9r1gxU &list.*

163 Manifesto of Hizb ut-Tahrir for Pakistan, "Pakistan, Khilafah and the Re-unification of the Muslim World," *http://www.hizb-pakistan.com/hizb/ index.php?option=com_content&view=article&id=837:manifesto-of-hizb-ut- tahrir-for-pakistan&catid=104:books&Itemid=487* (January 9, 2014).

164 Muhammad Amir Rana, "The Hizb ut Tahrir Threat," *Dawn,* July 11, 2011 (January 9, 2014).

fight from Pakistani soil. The Pakistani state lacks clarity in its approach to militant Islamism; Pakistan's politicians are often part of expedient political alignments with Islamist groups; and Pakistan's media allows Islamist views, including conspiracy theories, to prevail without allowing arguments against their beliefs to be amplified. As a result, Islamists with different strategies for acquiring political power continue to flourish in Pakistan while the writ of the state continues to weaken.[165]

Can I ask you to read that last line again, keeping in mind it was penned by the former ambassador from the country he is discussing, not some foreign journalist? Islamists will continue to *flourish* while the state continues to *weaken* – there is that tribalism again. We should all keep an eagle eye on the political and military developments in this crucial country. We can become obsessed with preventing a nuclear Iran, but a nuclear-Islamist Pakistan could be a larger and more real threat in the next few years. It might not take a violent coup to wrest the briefcase with nuclear codes from a secular government. It could happen quite peaceably at the ballot box or as a result of a routine promotion within the military.

Outside of the political machinations in Pakistan lie other routes for 120 to 130 nuclear warheads to end up in Islamist hands. In many of the emerging democracies in the world, when push comes to shove, the military still rules the country. The same is true in Pakistan, which is why nuclear scientists there worry about an internal transfer of nuclear authorization to high-ranking Islamist officers, either in public or in secret.

A recent book entitled *Confronting the Bomb: Pakistani and Indian Scientists Speak Out* would probably make your hair curl if you read all of its essays. Pakistani scientists, it turns out, are quite worried about the growing Islamist influence in the

165 *http://www.ctlibrary.com/ct/2006/june/29.38.html* (January 16, 2014).

military. Nuclear physicist and defense analyst Pervez Hoodbhoy, the book's editor, summarized the nervousness this way:

> Safety and security of Pakistan's nuclear arsenals is of a major concern. The growing radicalization within the military, given attacks on its own internal bases, could lead to these nuclear weapons being hijacked by radical Islamists. Hoodbhoy cites a change in Pakistani weapons development as another red flag: Earlier, such weapons (warheads) were seen just as a means of deterrence. The most dangerous development is the increasing search for fissile material as a new dimension of tactical nuclear war has entered the picture. This means the number of weapons will steadily increase.[166]

While the Pakistani military sees increasing Islamist influence, Muslim scholars have made possession of weapons of mass destruction an important topic of study and teaching in recent years. Scholars have published many papers on the correct, most Islamic approach to these weapons, and again, if you read these papers in detail, I guarantee you will feel a shiver run down your spine. Among the latest conclusions of respected religious scholars, a group that has far more weight in their governments than their cohorts in Western countries, are:

- Islam allows the accumulation of sufficient force to "terrorize the enemy and deter against an attack upon Muslims."

- The "prevention of Muslims from the production of weapons of mass destruction ... while other countries are allowed to do this – causes general, great and large damage upon all Muslims."

- It is thus permissible for Muslims to produce WMDs

"in order to seek balance in armed conflict between them and hostile forces." The achievement of strategic balance with the enemy is not only legitimate, but religiously obligatory.

- "It is possible for an Islamic state to use this type of weapon if the enemy uses it, or it is thought likely that the enemy is poised to use it."[167]

This is another section where I politely ask you to read the points above again. Chew on them awhile. Think about how you would respond if you were a Muslim military officer in Pakistan and you read: "The achievement of strategic balance with the enemy is not only legitimate, but religiously obligatory." Think about what you would feel if you were an Iranian nuclear physicist and read that the "prevention of Muslims from the production of weapons of mass destruction ... while other countries are allowed to do this – causes general, great and large damage upon all Muslims." Consider your reaction as a general, in either Pakistan or Iran, when you meditate on: "It is possible for an Islamic state to use this type of weapon if the enemy uses it, or it is thought likely that the enemy is poised to use it."

Do you understand that the pronouncements of Koranic scholars in the Muslim world are far more influential than anything the Pope or Billy Graham says in the Western world? There is no comparison. When recognized Islamic scholars speak, all Muslims listen. When those scholars state clearly that it is a *religious obligation* to produce nuclear weapons of mass destruction to ward off the infidels, and that Islam sanctions use of such weapons if "it is thought likely that the enemy is poised to use it," you can see why everyone in the world should be nervous about Islamists getting within a million miles of

167 http://selfscholar.wordpress.com/2013/09/17/radioactive-fatwas-the-growing-islamist-legitimization-of-nuclear-weapons/ (December 15, 2013).

nuclear weapons. Can you detect the easy justification of pressing the button if you surmise that India, Israel, or the U.S. *might* use a nuclear weapon? Military leaders in Islamic nations such as Pakistan have a convenient "out" if they launch a nuclear weapon. They have justified such a move in advance, simply adhering to sound Islamic doctrine.

Pakistan's politics and policies are as mysterious and difficult to discern as hieroglyphics, especially from a distance. United States intelligence services certainly do not seem to have a good read on Pakistan's backroom dealings, and if they can't figure out where this country is headed with hundreds of officers assigned full time to keep an eye on it, I will not pretend to know if and when Islamists will grab the nuclear briefcase. However, I think it's very safe to say that Islamism continues to gain strength in Pakistan, and as it does, the likelihood of jihadists getting access to the nuclear code rises. There is no evidence that I can find which suggests Pakistan is getting *less* Islamist with each passing year. In fact, the Islamist voices there are getting louder, and Islamists are winning a greater number of seats in Parliament.

As one Pakistani journalist recently said, "Nuclear programs are never safe. The Talibanization of the Pakistani military is something we can't overlook. What if there is an internal Taliban takeover of the nuclear assets?"[168] We not only ask this question in the U.S., but they are asking it in Pakistan as well. Whether these Islamists are inside or outside of the military, they seem to have an interesting habit of attacking bases that have nuclear weapons.[169] Up to this point, they have been repelled, but what happens if they break through? Ratcheting up the peril, many of the country's nuclear weapons are near to the heavily Islamist

---

168 *http://www.dw.de/why-pakistans-nuclear-bombs-are-a-threat/a-16730597* (December 15, 2013).

169 *http://www.nytimes.com/2012/08/17/world/asia/pakistani-air-force-base-with-nuclear-ties-is-attacked.html?_r=0* (January 28, 2014).

Swat Valley in-country.[170] Stridently Islamist voices ring out in every political campaign. Millions of Pakistanis echo those voices, and they would be thrilled to know that Islamists had obtained access to weapons of mass destruction and were ready to use them as a show of strength for Islam. Recent U.S. drone strikes in Pakistan have only poured fuel on the fire of Islamism within Pakistan and its army.[171]

As Gwynne Dyer, a respected journalist and observer of Pakistan, recently wrote from London: "A coup by Islamist officers in Pakistan would unleash the Mother of All Panics." He quoted an Indian Army officer as saying that "about six hours after news of an Islamist coup in Pakistan ... There would be a huge 'traffic jam' over Kahuta and other major Pakistani nuclear weapons facilities as the Indian, Iranian,

The likelihood of Islamists gaining access to the bomb has grown over the years.

American and Israeli air forces all tried to keep nuclear weapons out of the hands of the fanatics by destroying them." Such an attempt at obliterating the weapons before they could be used would not be successful, Dyer wrote, because the warheads are dispersed throughout the country.[172] The likelihood of Islamists gaining access to the bomb has grown over the years, Dyer added, because the Pakistani military has tolerated the diehards within its ranks, in exchange for relative peace in more conservative provinces. That "deal with the Devil" might backfire someday, with enormous consequences for global peace.

One wonders how long Islamism's rise in the military will be tolerated, and when the military will have a visible split into secular and fundamentalist camps. In little more than half a month as 2014 began, Pakistan witnessed forty-two terrorist

170 http://www.dw.de/why-pakistans-nuclear-bombs-are-a-threat/a-16730597.
171 http://smallwarsjournal.com/jrnl/art/the-growth-of-islamism-in-the-pak-istan-armym (December 16, 2013). A very good summary article on the power of Islamism within the Pakistani Army.
172 http://www.japantimes.co.jp/opinion/2012/01/30/commentary/islamist-mili-tary-coups-and-nuclear-weapons/ (December 15, 2013).

attacks in one province alone, including a bombing that killed twenty military members.[173] Just because we often don't read about these frequent attacks does not mean they are not occurring. We could very well wake up one day and learn about a definitive division within the military in Pakistan. The next step could be the Islamist side grabbing control of at least some of the nuclear weapons, if that does not happen peaceably prior to such a partition.

Now that we have considered two possible events which could unite and empower the Islamic world as never before, we turn to another possible gain of leverage for an Islamic bloc as it seeks to end centuries of global Western dominance: the Middle Eastern oil faucet being turned off as Islamists seize control of Saudi Arabia. Is there any evidence that such a radical change in Saudi society could occur? Let's take a look.

How Islamists Could Seize Control of Oil Reserves in Saudi Arabia

This has long been a point of speculation for observers of Saudi Arabia, primarily because they wonder how long a country can encourage a certain philosophy (Wahhabism, an ultra-strict interpretation of Islam) in schools, yet escape that philosophy's natural end – an overthrow of the ruling Saudi family to install a purely Islamic government and overhaul the entire society. Veteran Saudi experts are surprised it hasn't happened yet; others think that the House of Saud might continue to pull off its delicate balancing act of allowing Wahhabism to be taught to all age groups while maintaining tight control of power, and the oil reserves. The agreement between the House of Saud and ultra-conservative Muslims in the kingdom is described

---

173 *http://www.nytimes.com/2014/01/20/world/asia/pakistan.html?_r=0*
(January 20, 2014).

succinctly by Robert Baer, long-time CIA agent and observer of Saudi Arabia:

> *When King Abdullah's father Ibn Sa'ud founded Saudi Arabia in 1932, he came to a non-negotiable agreement with the Wahhabi religious establishment that, in return for allowing it control of the mosques, culture, and education, they would never go near core political issues, such as royal succession, foreign policy, and the armed forces. It's a deal that's been more or less respected for the last 80 years.*[174]

True, Saudi Arabia is probably not the oil well that it used to be and therefore struggles for power. It might not be as important to the world economy as previously thought. However, Saudi oil has long been the stabilizer of world oil prices, according to any oil market analyst, including the International Monetary Fund,[175] even if its reserves have dwindled and other nations are producing more oil or creating technologies such as fracking to get more out of the ground.[176] In addition, no new countries have arisen in recent years to ramp up oil production dramatically. Thus, we could easily say that as oil becomes scarcer worldwide, Saudi Arabia will have at least as much leverage as it does now. If experts such as former Secretary of Energy James Schlesinger are right and world oil production will peak in 2015, then Saudi Arabia will possess a large share of a meager resource. Since the 1970s, for example, every one barrel of newly discovered oil has been negated by three barrels pumped out of the ground, an untenable formula for continued expansion of production.[177]

The U.S. should be applauded for pouring billions of dollars

---

174 http://www.newrepublic.com/article/114468/why-saudi-arabia-helping-crush-muslim-brotherhood (January 20, 2014).
175 http://www.imf.org/external/pubs/ft/survey/so/2013/car072413a.htm (January 28, 2014).
176 http://alcalde.texasexes.org/2012/10/an-end-to-saudi-oil/ (December 10, 2013).
177 Ibid.

into alternative energy sources and developing fracking technology, which is short for hydraulic fracturing of rock via pressurized liquid, increasing the flow of petroleum and other resources into wells. Yet our nation and the rest of the West continue to be scarily dependent on oil. Even more dependent on Saudi and Iranian oil is China, the number-one importer of Middle Eastern oil, which would make it the first to succumb to an Islamic embargo.[178]

Any such stoppage of the oil from Saudi Arabia would bring most of the world to its knees with the threat of a collapse in the global economy. It's not a reach at all to picture a caliph declaring that no more oil will be exported from OPEC without each importer's agreement to "peace" pacts with the new caliphate. For those of you not old enough to remember what happens when the spigot shuts off, check your history books for the facts about OPEC's 1973 embargo, a huge event in world history, when Saudi Arabia cut off exports to the U.S. to protest our support of Israel in its war with Egypt and Syria. Gas prices soared, service station lines ballooned, and the entire economy plunged, temporarily. Fortunately, the export stoppage lasted just six months.[179]

Speculating on what would happen if the flow of petroleum was blocked from East to West, we must dig a little deeper into this question of how likely it is for Islamists to gain access to the Saudi oil fields.

A recent survey of twelve hundred foreign policy experts, government officials, and academics identified Saudi Arabia's "political instability" as a development to keep an eye on in 2014.[180] I wrote extensively about this scenario in my first book,

---

178 http://online.wsj.com/news/articles/SB100014241278873247551045790732839 48517714 (January 20, 2014).

179 http://www.npr.org/blogs/parallels/2013/10/15/234771573/the-1973-arab-oil-embargo-the-old-rules-no-longer-apply (January 27, 2014).

180 http://www.foreignpolicy.com/articles/2013/12/24/cloudy_with_a_chance_of_conflict (November 23, 2013).

drawing heavily from Baer's analysis of Saudi Arabia. I will cite a quote used in my previous work to illuminate the type of scene we could face:

> Take the rage in the mosques and the streets of Saudi Arabia, add weapons and a willingness to use them, not just against Western terrorist targets but against the House of Sa'ud and the petroleum infrastructure that supports it; continue to look the other way while it all happens, and we can take the last half century of oil-fired industrial prosperity and kiss it g-o-o-d-b-y-e.[181]

With the wind of the Arab Spring blowing throughout the Middle East, Saudi Arabia's royal family has probably spent time in prayer asking Allah to reverse the breeze before it hits the kingdom's borders. As Baer added in a recent article on why Saudi Arabia has given massive aid to Egypt after the ousting of President Morsi in July 2013:

> The Saudis watched in mute horror as Egypt's Arab Spring led to the legitimization of the Muslim Brotherhood in voting booths. They could only ask whether their turn was next. A source close to the Saudis told me, 'The royal family looks at the Muslim Brotherhood as hands down the most serious threat to its existence. Its Shia minority doesn't come even close.'[182]

I think democracy is a long way off for Saudi Arabia, and this third scenario of this chapter is the least likely to occur within the next few years. Yet I'm also sure that even expert analysts would not have predicted the rapid fall of dictators in Tunisia, Libya, and Egypt in the Arab Spring, especially as a result of a poor fruit vendor setting himself on fire. In fact, many journals

---

181   Robert Baer, *Sleeping with the Devil: How Washington Sold Our Soul for Saudi Crude* (New York, NY: Broadway Books, 2003), 11.

182   *http://www.newrepublic.com/article/114468/ why-saudi-arabia-helping-crush-muslim-brotherhood.*

continue to run articles that explain how analysts completely missed the signs of an Arab Spring.[183]

Even though the likelihood of Saudi Arabia falling to Islamists is somewhat remote, given its massive military budget (fifth in the world, behind only the U.S., Russia, Japan, and the U.K.)[184] and promised American help in case of trouble, a few troubling developments in the kingdom could be portents of unrest. All of these factors deserve to be tracked in coming years:

- Massive unemployment among young people – a fine piece of kindling to start a fire. How massive? Try 40 percent for people between the ages of fifteen and twenty-four, as reported in 2011. The government has responded to this crisis by promising more public-sector jobs and unemployment insurance, two stopgap measures that will not last forever.[185] The Saudis are racing against time as they wonder how long millions of unemployed men will accept state subsidies and unemployment insurance before they revolt.

- Food prices have risen in recent years, as has overall inflation, while at the same time the state subsidies to its citizens have declined. In other words, the economic numbers that indicate a healthy economy and stable society are going in opposite directions. Some Saudis even live at a poverty level, an incredible reality given the kingdom's oil wealth, which is not at all distributed evenly.[186]

- Not only is there a large class of poor young people,

183 http://www.foreignaffairs.com/articles/67932/f-gregory-gause-iii/why-middle-east-studies-missed-the-arab-spring (January 28, 2014).

184 http://www.mapsofworld.com/world-top-ten/world-top-ten-countries-with-largest-defence-budget-map.html (January 28, 2014).

185 http://www.bbc.co.uk/news/world-middle-east-12637765 (January 20, 2014).

186 http://www.npr.org/2011/02/24/134021440/little-unrest-but-growing-frustration-in-saudi (January 20, 2014).

but there are thousands upon thousands of university-educated young people returning from abroad to no jobs.[187] Thus, there is a potential leader class among the discontented that could direct a revolution through social media adeptness (see: Egypt) and at least theoretical expertise in running a government.

- Government leaders are considering further cuts to the generous subsidies that Saudi citizens enjoy. They pay less than fifty cents per gallon of gasoline and have subsidized water and electricity, in part to preserve the tenuous social order. More subsidies were promised as a result of the Arab Spring, but officials, such as the economy and planning minister, say these subsidies "distort" and ultimately slow the Saudi economy.[188] As oil reserves dwindle and the population continues to explode, Saudi Arabia will discover what many European nations have discovered in the past few years: a welfare state can only work for a limited amount of time. Eventually the population overwhelms the system and cuts have to be made – leading to intense anger in the streets.

Even with these troubling factors present, most analysts think change will come more slowly in Saudi Arabia than in other Arab countries because of its unique social composition. Thomas Lippman, an analyst at the Council on Foreign Relations and long-time observer of the kingdom, says revolution is not likely "because no one questions the legitimacy of the regime, and the king is personally popular ... The place is not stagnant as Egypt was. Everyone knows there is going to be change in

---

187 Ibid.
188 *http://www.ft.com/intl/cms/s/0/f474cf28-b717-11e2-841e-00144feabdc0.html#axzz2qxAIpJgA* (January 20, 2014).

the next few years" as older members of the royal family die, many of whom are in their eighties now.[189]

Other experts, such as Sandra Mackey, who have lived in Saudi Arabia for extended periods of time and written extensively about the kingdom, foresee a different possibility – the country breaking into regions as the central government implodes. That would, of course, make the oil fields far easier to plunder by a band of Islamists or an Islamic bloc to taunt the Western, infidel enemy with an embargo.

Mackey explains it this way:

> Those who depend on Saudi Arabia's oil hold an enormous stake in what happens. The Saudis as a whole remain too passive to rise up in revolt. Even if they gathered the energy and commitment to forcibly overthrow the House of Saud, they possess no ideology or institution capable of creating an alternative system of governance. Nor is there any foundation on which to build for the common good, because there is no concept among the Saudis of benefits for anyone beyond the family. That means that either the House of Saud remains too ineffective to preside over the deteriorating social fabric, which encompasses the military, or the country implodes. The kingdom's regions – the Hejaz, the Hasa, and the Nejd – spin off from each other followed by Asir, Jizan, and the northern frontier … Family and tribe look after their own. And greedy outsiders with powerful militaries gather to compete for the oil resources of the collapsed kingdom.[190]

I could scan websites and make a case for imminent upheaval in Saudi Arabia, but after hours of research, it appears that the

189 http://www.npr.org/2011/02/24/134021440/
     little-unrest-but-growing-frustration-in-saudi.
190 http://nationalinterest.org/commentary/saudi-arabias-road-implosion-
     9051?page=2 (January 20, 2014).

Arab Spring will not bloom in the kingdom anytime soon. Of course, that does not mean that a Facebook campaign will not convince millions of unemployed men and women in Saudi to hit the streets tomorrow. For now, the royal family has tried to respond to troubling demographics by increasing housing opportunities and unemployment insurance, among other measures, to keep the populace somewhat fat and happy. I do think that this idea of the kingdom fracturing into several regions bears watching, especially as members of the shrewd royal family die in the next few years and unknown future leadership leads either well or poorly.

Whether or not Islamists grab control of Saudi oil, the huge reserves there could be conscripted to aid the goals of the final caliph. There is always the possibility of a large Muslim bloc of countries staring down Saudi Arabia, no matter who is in charge, and ordering it to give them control of oil for the spread of the kingdom of Allah. I will expand on this scenario in the next chapter.

Somehow, some way, I think Saudi oil wealth will be a blue chip bargaining tool for the Antichrist, the new caliph. What does Islamic prophecy say about this man? Let's take a brief look at what I reported in my first book, along with recent statements made about this man in the nine years that have intervened.

Who Will Unite Muslims and Take On the West?

What kind of leader would be needed to unite an extremely disparate group of Muslims around the world, tired of Western domination and seeking earnestly to "prepare" the world for Allah's final judgment as the "last, best revelation of God" is presented to all? This man would have to have unusual gifts of diplomacy, holiness, charm, wisdom, and the ability to gain the admiration and respect of Muslims worldwide.

Well, you should know that Muslims are already waiting

for this man, with 42 percent in a recent survey believing the Islamic superman will appear in their lifetime.[191] His name is al-Mahdi, the "Rightly Guided One," who has been discussed since the earliest days of Islam. This Islamic messiah was referred to by Muhammad's grandson, Ali, who said that Islam would "prevail over all religions ... when the Messiah of this *ummah* (Islamic nation) makes his appearance."[192] The topic of Mahdi has drawn more interest from the Shia branch of Islam, probably because the prophet purportedly said that Mahdi would come from his clan, an endorsement of the Shia view that the caliphate should have remained in Muhammad's family tree. Despite a greater emphasis on Mahdi in Shiite literature, he has been discussed by all branches of Islam throughout history, as revealed by this quote from what has been called the greatest Islamic history book from the pre-modern era:

> Let it be known that it is a narrated event by ALL Muslims in EVERY era that at the end of time a man from the family of the Prophet (PBUH&HF) will, without fail, make his appearance and will strengthen Islam and spread justice; Muslims will follow him and he will gain domination over the Muslim realm. He will be called al-Mahdi.[193]

Dozens of books have been written about Mahdi, including at least forty-six by thirty-five Sunni scholars,[194] and many others penned by Shiite teachers, the smaller sect of Islam. Mahdi (also Mehdi or Maadi; the vowels are flexible in Arabic) will appear just as mankind reaches a stage of great suffering, to

---

191 *http://www.mahdiwatch.org/* (January 28, 2014). This is a fascinating site if you want to keep an eye out for Mahdi.

192 Ed Hotaling, *Islam without Illusions: Its Past, Its Present, and Its Challenges for the Future* (Syracuse, NY: Syracuse University Press, 2003), 102.

193 Ibn Khaldun, *The Muqaddimah: An Introduction to History* (Princeton, NJ: Princeton University Press, 1967), 257-58.

194 *http://www.al-islam.org/shiite-encyclopedia-ahlul-bayt-dilp-team/sunni-documentation-imam-al-mahdi* (December 20, 2013).

show the light of Islam when men and women need it most, and to prepare the world for Allah's judgment just in time, according to accepted Islamic teaching.[195] Mahdi will accomplish this by leading an exemplary Islamic life of submission, and inspiring the faithful to do the same. Muslims have always believed in the correlation between holy living and military triumph, which leads to the expansion of the ummah. Mahdi will be far more than a gifted teacher; he will also be

Muslims have always believed in the correlation between holy living and military triumph.

a brilliant military commander, in some ways a modern-day reincarnation of the prophet. One writer predicts: "The Mahdi will establish right and justice in the world and eliminate evil and corruption. He will fight against the enemies of the Muslims who would be victorious."[196]

Given that many of the world's most corrupt countries are Islamic (eight of the top ten),[197] this impeccable integrity in Mahdi will be a welcome relief to many. He is praised more for his morality than any other aspect of his character, as you read Islamic teaching about him. His total submission to Allah will lead to incredible triumph on the battlefield. As another writer has said:

> He will reappear on the appointed day, and then he will fight against the forces of evil, lead a world revolution and set up a new world order based on justice, righteousness and virtue ... ultimately the righteous will take the world administration in their hands and Islam will be victorious over all the religions.[198]

---

195 Ibn Kathir, *The Signs Before the Day of Judgment* (London: Dar Al-Taqwa Ltd., 1991).

196 Sideeque M. A. Veliankode, *Doomsday: Portents and Prophecies* (Scarborough, Canada: Al-Attique, 1999), 4-5.

197 http://www.businessinsider.com/the-most-corrupt-countries-in-the-world-2013-12 (January 20, 2014).

198 Ayatullah Baqir al-Sadr and Ayatullah Murtadha Mutahhari, *The Awaited Saviour* (Karachi, Pakistan: Islamic Seminary Publications, 2013), 4-5.

If this sounds like the Antichrist, you can see why many of us who have studied Islam for years believe that Mahdi will be that man. One Muslim Background Believer who has done a lot of speaking and writing about al-Mahdi, Walid Shoebat, says that as he read scriptural prophecy for the first time, he was astonished by the description of the Antichrist. His conclusion? This is the Mehdi that we have long talked about in Islam.[199]

Other aspects of Mahdi's profile include:

- He will be from the line of Fatimah, Muhammad's first wife, and become a public figure at age forty.[200] Physically, he will have a high forehead and hooked nose, according to prophecies traced back to Muhammad.[201]

- He will center his operations in Karbala, Iraq, according to Shiites. A hadith of Muhammad says that he will sweep across the Middle East and set up his reign in Jerusalem.[202] That reign will, of course, be headquartered at the Dome of the Rock, the mosque in Jerusalem that forbids Christians and Jews to enter it. Tourists are allowed to spend one hour at the site, but if thought to be praying, are ushered immediately off the outer grounds. The Dome of the Rock is always understood to have Last Days implications for Muslims.[203]

- He will have miracle-working power, which will impress the Islamic community and verify his status as a special instrument of Allah. One teaching says, "In the Last

199 http://www.youtube.com/watch?v=SkPC2Sus_IU, one of several videos on this topic (January 12, 2014).
200 Sunan Abu Dawud, Book 36, Number 4271, narrated by Umm Salamah, ummul Mu'minin.
201 http://islamqa.info/en/13818 (December 22, 2013).
202 http://www.answering-islam.org/Authors/JR/Future/ch04_the_mahdi.htm (December 22, 2013).
203 Gulru Necipoglu, "The Dome of the Rock as Palimpset: Abd al-Malik's Grand Narrative and Sultan Suyleman's Glosses," in Muqarnas, vol. 25 (Boston: Brill, 2008), 81.

Days of the ummah, the Mahdi will appear. Allah will give him power over the wind and the rain, and the earth will bring forth its foliage."[204]

- He will guide Muslims to great wealth, but he will not lead a profligate lifestyle. Instead, he "will give away wealth profusely, flocks will be in abundance, and the ummah will be large and honored."[205] Likewise, "A man will stand and say, 'Give to me Mahdi!' and he will say, 'Take.'"[206]

- He will rule over the world for seven years, according to most accounts, including those that claim to trace this time span back to Muhammad's prediction.[207] This will feature a seven-year "peace agreement" between the "Arabs and the Romans," what many believe will be between Islam and the West. Such parallels with Scripture are no accident, according to many.

- He will be assisted by "Jesus," who will descend, probably in Damascus, from heaven to work miracles and preach Islam. "Jesus will testify against those who had called him son of God, the Christians, and those who had belied him, the Jews."[208] I think this Islamic version of Jesus fits the description of the Antichrist's assistant in Revelation 13 perfectly. While Mahdi straightens out the ummah by "freeing Islam from the hypocrites

204 Sheik Muhammad Hisham Kabbani, *The Approach of Armageddon? An Islamic Perspective* (Canada: Islamic Supreme Council of America, 2003), 233.
205 Ibid.
206 Muhammad ibn Izzat, Muhammad Arif, *Al Mahdi and the End of Time* (London: Dar Al-Taqwa, 1997), 9.
207 *http://islamqa.info/en/13818* (December 22, 2013).
208 Mufti Mohammad Shafi Usmani, *Signs of the Qiyamah and the Arrival of the Maseeh* (Karachi, Pakistan: Darul Ishat, 2000), 60.

who have corrupted it," this Jesus will handle the evan-
gelization of the Jewish and Christian communities.[209]

The end result? "Jesus" will summon Christians and Jews
"to live by the Qu'ran by purging them of the errors into which
they have fallen. As Christians follow the Prophet Isa [Jesus],
the Christian and Islamic world will unite in a single belief,
and the world will enjoy a period of great peace, security, hap-
piness, and well-being, known as the Golden Age."[210]

Here is a fitting capstone to describe al-Mahdi:

> *He is the precursor of the victory of the Truth and the*
> *fall of all tyrants. He heralds the end of injustice and*
> *oppression and the beginning of the final rising of the*
> *sun of Islam which will never again set and which will*
> *ensure happiness and the elevation of mankind ... The*
> *Mahdi is one of Allah's clear signs which will soon be*
> *made evident to everyone.*[211]

And, he will rule from Jerusalem, according to a hadith
from Muhammad:

> *Jerusalem will be the location of the rightly guided*
> *caliphate and the center of Islamic rule, which will be*
> *headed by Imam al-Mahdi ... that will abolish the lead-*
> *ership of the Jews ... and put an end to the domination*
> *of the Satans who spit evil into people and cause cor-*
> *ruption in the earth, making them slaves of false idols*
> *and ruling the world by laws other than the sharia of the*
> *Lord of the worlds.*[212]

There is, of course, no guarantee that these Islamic prophecies will come true. They are not from an infallible source.

---

209 *http://www.awaitedmahdi.com/mahdi01.html* (November 15, 2013).
210 Ibid.
211 Muhammad ibn Izzat, Muhammad Arif, *Al Mahdi and the End of Time*
     (London: Dar Al-Taqwa, 1997), 4.
212 Ibid.

However, if the entire Islamic world is looking for this type of person, I think it will be eager to anoint someone to fill this role. It is not a stretch to imagine this Islamic figure leading a bloc of Muslim nations in conquest of Israel, something that Scripture talks about – an Antichrist invading the Holy Land. I can see this ruler daring the world to react to his *What other faith or philosophy has such a stake in Jerusalem? None.* bold move, and it's surely no accident that Muslims consider the Dome of the Rock in Israel one of their holiest sites. What other faith or philosophy has such a stake in Jerusalem? None.

People who have dedicated years to researching Mahdi believe that the time is ripe for his appearance. One man who has written a book on Mahdism and has a Ph.D. in history gives the reasons for this:

Mahdism is, historically, closely tied to belief in the mujaddid, the "renewer" of Islam predicted in several hadith to come every 100 years; thus, eschatological expectations in Islam have tended to skyrocket as the turn of each Muslim century approaches, as was the case in 1979 (al-Utaybi), 1881 (the Sudanese Mahdi), etc. The year 1500 AH (After Hijra) will occur in 2076 A.D. Couple that with the empirical data from Pew indicating strong eschatological beliefs among many Muslims, the global Islamic community's growing sense of victimization at the hands of the Christian West (and Russia), the burgeoning influence of transnational Islamic movements ... as well as the continued (indeed, flourishing) popularity and power of jihad-waging terrorist groups – and the emergence of a political and/or military Mahdist movement in the coming decades appears to be a good bet.[213]

213 http://www.mahdiwatch.org/index.html.

I could write pages more on this quote, but suffice it to say that even if 99.9 percent of American Christians have never heard of the Mahdi, nearly 700 million Muslims are eagerly awaiting him. What kind of man will he be? From what nationality or people group? People often ask me for my guesses of specific people as the Mahdi, and I do not dare to answer. That's a tough prognostication, and I would hate to label anyone incorrectly. I do, however, have an idea of *where* he will come from, and more prophecy scholars are pointing to one country as *the* key nation in the End Times. That's what chapter 5 is all about.

CHAPTER FIVE

One Key Nation to Watch

Now that we have established the type of events that need to occur to unite the Islamic world and have learned about the leader Muslims are waiting for to steer a bloc of nations in a resurrection of the caliphate, we need to ponder what country could emerge as a home base for this new powerhouse. Speculation on this topic might be little more than a crapshoot, but let me illustrate one plausible picture. I know *for certain* that events will occur in the next five years that no one saw coming. I know that because in my first book, I hardly mentioned Iran or Turkey; eight years later, I am basing my latest conjecture on a framework in which those countries play lead roles. In a few more years, perhaps we will all be convinced that Libya and Jordan are the key countries in the world. Change occurs very, very rapidly in the twenty-first century, and upheavals in the Islamic world occur on an almost daily basis in places we do not expect. For example, did you foresee the Arab Spring or Syria's civil war?

I am not going to say in this chapter that Turkey will definitively be the cradle of the Antichrist, but I can make an airtight argument that this country is worth keeping a *very close* eye on. I came a little late to the "Turkey is a key country" party, but now that I have arrived, I am sounding the trumpet.

Sure, I have a certain bias, having lived there for a couple of years. It's an absolutely fascinating place, loaded with history, political intrigue, outstanding food, an interesting culture, and an abundance of riches. There is bountiful produce of all types, mountains, beautiful beaches, vibrant cities, and miles and miles of rolling hills and towns that seem straight out of biblical times – in fact, they are. I could write an advertisement for Turkish tourism pretty easily, but I'll spare you the details.

I will tell you this: Christians who have lived in Turkey as tent-making missionaries speak in the same way about the country that I do. While they are not 100 percent sure how Turkey will factor into the End Times, they are certain that

"Because I think this is where it is all going to go down." it will play a key part. I will never forget talking to one of these long-time residents on a pay phone in Istanbul a few years ago. Hundreds of people passed by on the sidewalk of a busy street in the historic district, just a block from the Blue Mosque, as I raised my voice to be heard and asked this woman a dozen questions about her ministry. My wife and I were on an exploratory trip to Turkey at the time, soaking in a brand new country and culture. On a cool, cloudy afternoon as my wife waited patiently on a bench, I asked my new friend point-blank: "Why have you stayed in this country despite the difficulties? Tell me about your calling to this place." She answered immediately, "Because I think this is where it is all going to go down." I paused in astonishment and felt goose bumps all over my body. I heard a certainty in that voice, a total lack of hesitation based on twenty-plus years of experience in-country. All I could say was, "Really?"

The hunches of a few cross-cultural workers are not enough to build a thesis on. I'm sure workers in other countries feel the same way, particularly in Iran, Iraq, Jordan, or any number of places. I do find it interesting, however, that more and more prophecy speculators are zeroing in on Turkey as the key country in the End Times, as any Google search will reveal. This chapter will make an argument for this country playing a central role in the fulfillment of biblical prophecy. Let's have a look.

"My Grandfather Cut Off Their Grandfathers' Heads"

The discussion in our classroom, which hosted some of Turkey's best and brightest high school minds, turned to the European opinion of the Turkish republic as we discussed the impact of history in our acquisition of knowledge. We interacted about how the hundreds of years of conflict between the Ottoman Empire and the continent undoubtedly impacted the discussions of the European Union (EU) to allow Turkey into its exclusive club. As I voiced my pessimism about the EU ever admitting Turkey, one of my students piped up: "That's okay, Mr. Stice. My grandfather cut off their grandfathers' heads." There was a light chuckle among the students, a knowing laugh that Turks a few generations ago had indeed killed colonialist Europeans seeking a slice of Anatolia, and centuries before had made major inroads into Europe's kingdoms.

If you have never been to Turkey or have never even thought about the country, I do not blame you at all for not caring about this nation on the rise or for being ignorant of its incredible history. I knew a bit about the country before teaching there, had read a few books and interacted with a few Turks, but it was not until I got there that I realized just how important its history is to the people – and their not-so-subtle desire to repeat that history and restore the former glory of their nation. Whether or not you have been a student of the Ottoman Empire, the facts about this gigantic spread of Islam into areas where it had never ventured between the thirteenth and twentieth centuries still astound:

- It must be called the most powerful empire in the world during the sixteenth and seventeenth centuries, stretching from southeastern Europe all the way to the Horn of Africa, overseeing thirty-two provinces and other vassal states, ruling thirty million people over three continents, and being compared to the Roman Empire in terms of political and military success.[214]

- This empire spread Islam and Turkish culture from Austria to Saudi Arabia, and the Turks oversaw the holy sites of Islam for centuries, as well as territory from Russia to Algeria at its height from 1683 to 1699.

- For six centuries, it was acknowledged as the fulcrum between the East and West, ruling the Mediterranean Sea and controlling many world trade routes. Turkish leaders are blunt today about the country recapturing its primacy as a link between East and West.

- The empire's motto was "The Eternal State," and many Christians in the centuries of its rule firmly believed it to be the embodiment of the Antichrist. This idea gained added traction when the bulwark of eastern Christianity, Constantinople, was conquered in 1453 (a year more important to Turks than 1492 is to North Americans!). This city's capture cannot be overstated as a turning point in Islamic history. Many credible Islamic sources indicate that Muhammad predicted its downfall at the hand of Muslims,[215] but the transformation of one of Christianity's most stunning cathedrals into a mosque was an incredible achievement, especially given the legendary impenetrability of the city's walls.[216] You can look at this conquest as a simple movement of history, but Muslims to this day see it as a miracle and

---

214 Deringil, Selim, "The Turks and 'Europe': The Argument from History," *Middle Eastern Studies*, Vol. 43, No. 5 (September 2007): 709-723.

215 http://www.answering-christianity.com/prophecies_by_prophet_muhammad.htm (October 5, 2014).

216 http://lostislamichistory.com/mehmed-ii-and-the-prophets-promise/ (January 21, 2014).

a vital beachhead that they established in the Western world, never to be surrendered, a symbolic crushing of the Christian god. You can find many, many sources in which Europeans called Turks "the Antichrist" as they expanded their territory and fought brutally to defend the Holy Land from the Crusaders.[217] If you were huddled in Constantinople in 1453, you would have certainly believed that the End Times were upon you. In other words, what I am writing in this chapter is not at all a new idea. Furthermore, the Turkish sultans of this era believed that they were the agents of Allah to prepare the world for final judgment as they spread Islam farther than it had ever gone. As one Italian who visited with Sultan Mehmet, the conqueror of Constantinople, said of him:

He is at great pains to learn the geography of Italy ... where the seat of the pope is and that of the emperor, and how many kingdoms there are in Europe ... He burns with desire to dominate ... It is with such a man that we Christians have to deal ... Today, he says, the times have changed, and declares that he will advance from east to west as in former times the Westerners advanced into the Orient. There must, he says, be only one empire, one faith, and one sovereignty in the world.[218]

Were it not for some fascinating historical occurrences

---

217 *http://books.google.com/books?id=UH1JHVZsLgC&pg=PA142&lpg=PA142& dq=turks+as+the+antichrist+in +the+middle+ages&source=bl&ots=rEmb7Y JiEh&sig=8Naut2Z2EU6CNyeq-0vGbCkm2q4&hl=en&sa= X&ei=jYXeUuv- F5HMsQSWlILACw&ved=0CEoQ6AEwBzgK#v=onepage&q=turks percen- t20as percent20the percent20antichrist percent20in percent20the percent- 20middle percent20ages&f=false* (January 21, 2014), a good example of the evolution of how Westerners viewed Muslims in the Middle Ages.

218 Roger Crowley, *1453: The Holy War for Contantinople and the Clash of Islam and the West* (New York, NY: Hyperion, 2005), 45.

in 1529, 1532, and 1683, when the Turks failed to conquer Vienna, the sultans after Mehmet might have achieved their goal.

- Few people realize this, but the Ottoman Empire ruled Jerusalem for four hundred years, from 1517 to 1917, and actually permitted a surprising freedom of worship for Christians and Jews in the Holy City.

But it is not my intention to make this book a historical study. You can find abundant websites and books on the glories of the Ottoman Empire. What I want to convey is during the years we know as the Middle Ages, the Renaissance, and even the Industrial Revolution, which we studied so diligently during our school years, there was a looming giant in the backyard of Michelangelo and Voltaire, da Vinci and Dickens – the behemoth of the Ottoman Empire. A short look eastward from 1300 to 1900 reveals a feared fighting force, legendary for its discipline and ruthlessness. For Muslims, it was a time when Islam flourished, as it was reinterpreted by the Turks, and included some of the greatest scientific discoveries in history and expansions in the arts.

The Nation Thought To Be the Antichrist for Hundreds of Years

We Americans might be ignorant of the scope and length of the Ottoman Empire, but Europeans sure aren't. They grow up learning about the "horrible, bloodthirsty" Turks who tromped all over their fair continent and cut off people's heads, raped their women, and tried to convert everyone to their religion. As Geoffrey Woodward points out in his article in the magazine *History Today* entitled "The Ottomans in Europe," the kingdom at its peak made many a European quiver with fear:

> *The Ottoman army was the largest in Europe, its navy*

ruled the shipping lanes in the eastern Mediterranean,
and its capital Istanbul was five times the size of Paris.
Its resources seemed limitless, and its capacity to sweep
aside opposition in the name of Islam gave the Turkish
Empire an awesome presence. Indeed between 1520 and
1565 its momentum seemed unstoppable.[219]

You don't have to look far to see the impact the Turks made on Europeans, both physically and psychologically. You'll see veiled women, and men with black hair and mustaches all over Europe, descendants of Turks who settled in the Empire's far provinces. Where do you think the Muslims in Bosnia, for example, came from? They did not spring out of Bosnian soil. The sons and daughters of the Ottomans spread Islam all over Europe long before Europeans became afraid of immigrant reproduction in places like France, England, and Spain. Eastern Europe in particular is filled with Turks, and Germany has a mammoth Turkish population of at least four million. I know from personal experience you can go into just about any restaurant in Vienna today and hear Turkish spoken. Turks can be found in dozens of European countries, a testament to the far reach of the Ottoman Empire.

My wife and I took a memorable train ride on the Orient Express westward a couple of years ago. It was fascinating for us to pass towns in Bulgaria, Serbia, and Hungary, and to see the descendants of the Turks living in those countries. Bulgaria was a country of stark contrast – when you receive change there, the coins have Jesus holding a cross on them, but your change might be handed to you by a Muslim Turk. You can see entire towns that appear to be primarily, if not entirely, comprised of Turks.

As you look around in some of the other countries along

---

219 *http://www.historytoday.com/geoffrey-woodward/ottomans-europe*
(December 20, 2013).

the route of the Orient Express, you see further reminders of the Empire's former sway. In Budapest, we looked at churches erected on pillars decorated not with images of the disciples, Moses, or David, but rather with Hungarian warriors killing Turks. We then came to discover that the church was established soon after the Turks had been expelled from Hungary in 1686. The history of Turks all over Europe is not ancient history to Europeans, trust me. And, if you don't think this has a huge impact on the EU's debate over whether or not to admit Turkey, you either don't know your history or have seriously underestimated its impact.

The theory of the Antichrist coming out of Turkey was one that European Christians not only could believe today, once they moved past their political correctness, *but one they've held to for centuries.* Martin Luther was one of many theologians who believed the Ottoman Empire had been allowed by God to "chastise Christians."[220] The tendency to believe this notion does not make it any truer. I'm simply trying to convey that a spirit of the Antichrist has been felt in Europe for centuries, and the origin of that spirit was Turkey. I do not want to demonize an entire country or its people. I love many Turks dearly and have an appreciation for their culture. The students I worked with were probably the most intelligent and winsome I have ever encountered, and I had many delightful Turkish colleagues. However, I am clear-eyed enough to know that many Turkish political leaders (and citizens) have grandiose ambitions in the modern world. I am simply saying that an empire which came close to world domination under one non-Christian ruler has already existed in Europe, and its name was the Ottoman Empire.

---

220 *http://www.prophezine.com/index.php?option=com_
   content&view=article&id=690:gog-as-antichrist-a-historical-
   survey&catid=41:top-headlines* (December 12, 2013).

Turks and the Middle East

In the other direction, eastward, Turks ruled the bulk of the Middle East, including the holiest sites of Islam, and only lost these treasures about a century ago, during World War I. Early in my stay in Turkey, my Turkish friends would often ask me, "Mr. Stice, when was the last time the Middle East was at peace?" I would hesitate with my response. They noticed this and would quickly reply, "When we ruled it." They would then add, every time, "So we need to rule it again." I was never sure how to respond to that opinion, which came from high school students and middle-aged adults.

To make a dangerous and sweeping generalization, Turks view Arabs as inferior to them. My students would come back from model UN field trips to Qatar and Israel saying they were completely unimpressed by Arab ways and people, calling them dirty and primitive, and lucky to have any influence in the world at all. Grudgingly, they admitted the Arabs' elevated status in the world, but ascribed it to only one thing: oil wealth. "Were it not for oil, Mr. Stice, those Bedouins would be filthy shepherds," my students would crow.

This is a common Turkish attitude towards Arabs, and it reflects a belief that I think many Turks have, even if they don't admit it: "The world was much better off with us in charge, and it would be better off today if we were to regain control of our former territories." This might sound absurd to some of my readers, who know nothing about Turkey and rarely hear the nation referred to when countries on the rise are discussed, such as China and India. But what many Americans don't realize is that Turkey has the fastest-growing economy in Europe, just behind China and India, according to some measures. That's why *Businessweek* called Turkey a "miracle."[221] In just the past

---

221 *http://www.businessweek.com/articles/2013-06-06/the-turmoil-behind-the-turkish-economic-miracle* (December 20, 2013).

decade, the per capita income has risen almost four times![222] Imagine how you would feel if the U.S. experienced such growth. When you go to Turkey these days, you can see this mushrooming growth everywhere you turn –

Turkey is booming, and the healthier it gets, the more it wants its empire back. endless cranes building apartment complexes, malls, mosques, schools, and all sorts of other structures. Turkey is booming, and the healthier it gets, the more it wants its empire back.

Some political scientists, even in the U.S., see the restoration of the Ottoman Empire as a welcome change to bring stability to the Middle East. Professor Emeritus of Political Science at Rutgers University Michael Curtis summarized this idea:

> *Arabs, living in these unstable and divided artificial countries created by colonial powers, must by this time surely regret the end of the Ottoman Empire that brought them safety and peace, if not democracy and civil rights. Surely the rest of the world, faced with endless conflicts among Arab states and by the growing Islamist threat, would be eager to agree to a restoration and to the accompanying addition of a stable and democratic Israel.[223]*

My Turkish friends could not have stated this any better – except for the inclusion of Israel!

Visualization of Restored Glory From the Top: "Nobody Will or Can Limit Our Vision"

This isn't just some pipe dream of a fish seller in Istanbul. Turkey's highest leaders make opaque and direct references to Turkey

---

222 Address to Brookings Institution, Washington, D.C., 11/18/2013, of Turkish Foreign Minister H.E. Ahment Davutoğlu, transcript retrieved at *http:// www.brookings.edu/~/media/events/2013/11/18%20turkey% 20davuto- glu/20131118_turkey_davutoglu_transcript.pdf* (December 20, 2013).

223 *http://www.americanthinker.com/2013/06/bring_back_the_ottoman_empire. html* (July 8, 2013).

restoring its former glory someday, becoming THE key power player in the Middle East vis-à-vis the West, at worst. One prime example of this vision occurred when powerful, charismatic Prime Minister Recep Tayyip Erdoğan was re-elected in 2011 by the largest margin ever for an incumbent prime minister. He made pointed references to former outposts of the Ottoman Empire in an acceptance speech that the media saw as code: "Believe me, Sarajevo won today as much as Istanbul, Beirut won as much as Izmir, Damascus won as much as Ankara, Ramallah, Nablus, Jenin, the West Bank, Jerusalem won as much as Diyarbakir."[224]

Much analysis has been devoted to this famous line, which received huge coverage abroad. I don't think it's very difficult to understand. Erdoğan was basically saying that Sarajevo still yearns to be Turkish, Damascus would be better off under Ottoman rule and Jerusalem will again one day belong completely to Muslims, under Turkish leadership. You can either look at Erdoğan's quote as one from a delusional madman, or from someone sly as a fox. Whatever your opinion, you should take careful note of the vision of this leader.

There are many, many other examples of the Turkish government seeing its country as a true global power and leader. One book that received wide coverage in Europe and the Middle East but is hardly ever mentioned in the U.S., was Foreign Minister H. E. Ahmet Davutoğlu's work, *Strategic Depth: Turkey's International Position,* which outlined the country's aspiration to be the strategic nation of the twenty-first century.[225] Davutoğlu asserted this Turkish pride and confidence in a recent address to the Brookings Institution in Washington, D.C.

---

224 *http://theoptimisticconservative.wordpress.com/2011/06/13/erdogan-ottoman-echoes-growing-louder/* (December 20, 2013).
225 *http://www.amazon.com/Stratejik-Derinlik-T%C3%BCrkiyenin-Uluslararasi-Konumu/dp/B004LYNDEQ/ref=sr_1_4?s=books&ie=UTF8&qid=1389558969&sr=1-4&keywords=ahmet+davutoğlu* (January 13, 2014).

He said that if Turkey had been allowed to join the European Union in 2003, "I am sure today we would have a new Europe, a much more creative, dynamic Europe, even responding to the economic crisis in a much better way."[226] The joke in Turkey now is they are very glad that the EU did *not* allow them to join their club, because the economic crises of Greece, Spain, Portugal, and others would have simply dragged down Turkey's explosive growth.

Can you see the chutzpah of Davutoğlu's statement, that Europe would be "much more dynamic" with Turkey included? Again, whether you consider him delusional or insightful, you need to notice the pride in his outlook. Regardless of what we think in the Western world about Turkey, Turks believe their country to be primed for world leadership, whether or not it is allowed into the good ol' boys club of the G8 or EU, or any other group you want to pick. Turks are well aware of why Europe does not like them, but it will not let a barricade in Brussels stop them from finding what they believe to be their rightful place in the world. Turkey is determined to find its way in a new global order that is being shaken every day. Do not be at all surprised if Turkey leads an Islamic federation one day and says, "We tried to join with you in the West, but you ungraciously snubbed us. We have joined a new club now and demand an equal say in how the world will proceed."

That is the primary thesis of this chapter. Having spent two years interacting with Turks of all ages, including government workers, extremely wealthy businesspeople, and the sons and daughters of politicians, I can tell you that the Turks believe deeply in their hearts that they are not only worthy of being a world power, but that the world would be a much better place

226 *http://www.taccenter.org/index.php?option=com_content&view=article&id=90&Itemid=292&lang=en* (January 13, 2014).

if they helped to run it. There is an unmistakable Turkish confidence, and you underestimate it at your own risk.

As Davutoğlu said in late 2013, in front of a room full of Americans about Turkey's desire to join the EU: "But that did not happen and nobody can blame Turkey." While waiting, the foreign minister pointed out, Turkey has been busy signing all sorts of trade and political agreements with thirty-five nations around it, opening thirty-six new embassies and strengthening ties with Russia, Iran, Iraq, Greece, and other countries. Davutoğlu also gave some insight into his schedule, mentioning summits with Afghanistan and Pakistan, Bosnia and Serbia. I can assure you that Turkey believes it is the natural leader for all of these nations if and when they form a coalition, a context that I tried to describe in the previous chapter.

Davutoğlu added that Turkey had representation in 221 nations, making it the seventh most widespread country in terms of foreign missions in the world, and of course, the only Islamic one in the top ten! "We will continue these openings because we want Turkey to be not only a regional power influential in surrounding regions, but a global player everywhere in the world." He wrapped up the final portion of his speech with these memorable lines:

> Therefore, we will be everywhere, whenever we are needed. We will be active everywhere. Some people may think – they may try to imagine or force us to be busy only with Syria, but in the morning we wake up with Syria, before noon our mind is in Balkans, in the afternoon, in Africa, in the evening in UN or in Latin America. Nobody will or can limit our vision.[227]

Is there any question as to how Mr. Davutoğlu and other Turkish leaders see their role? "We will be everywhere." "Nobody

---

227 Ibid.

will or can limit our vision." These quotes are, as they say, straight from the horse's mouth.

He went on to add that Turkey has robustly supported the nations of the Arab Spring, believing that only through democracy could true freedom flourish. He chided the West for not providing any economic support to the new governments in the Middle East, knowing full well that the U.S. and its allies could not possibly bankroll the very Islamists they are fighting in other parts of the world. Who is going to enforce some sort of order in these chaotic countries? Davutoğlu asked. The UN? He is making a case from silence that Turkey is the country that should be helping these countries learn democracy, with Islamist-leaning governments much like the one found in Turkey. If we hope that "some autocratic leaders will bring security and stability in the Middle East, it will be a big, big mistake," Davutoğlu added.[228]

I don't think there's any way you could walk out of that meeting in Washington, D.C., and not think one of two thoughts: 1) This is THE country to watch in the next ten to twenty years, or 2) That little guy had way more hubris than proof about his nation's importance. After the statements I found in his transcript, it was one or the other. Whenever an important government official makes bombastic statements about his country, we either have to conclude he is severely deceived or he knows something we don't.

Propaganda and "Inter-Faith Dialogue"

Perhaps Davutoğlu was so bold because he was speaking just a few miles from the construction site of what will be the largest Islamic complex in the Western hemisphere, the $100 million mega-mosque being erected in nearby Lanham, Maryland. The

228 http://www.brookings.edu/~/media/events/2013/11/18%20turkey%20davuto-glu/20131118_turkey_davutoglu_ transcript.pdf (December 10, 2013).

Turkish American Community Center will feature an exhibi-
tion hall, amphitheater, library, cultural center, athletic fields,
and a stunning mosque, among other structures.[229] Erdoğan
has visited the construction zone and sees it as a bulwark to
fight "Islamophobia" in the U.S.[230]

Turkey has made all sorts of inroads in the U.S. and other
Western countries, from sponsoring essay contests in schools
that yield a free trip to Turkey,[231] to a network
of dozens of schools with a core philosophy
of conservative Islamic values with a Turkish
slant, as I will discuss below. Ten years ago, I would venture
that Turkey had minimal exposure in the U.S. Today, you can
find Turkish talk shows on many cable channels, and Turkey
is constantly in the news, either for its political drama, urban
protests, or spectacular business expansion throughout the
Middle East. One key phrase to watch for as you see Turkey
ease its way onto the American radar is "inter-faith dialogue."
It is said to be a hallmark of the many Turkish schools that have
been founded in the U.S. over the past decade, and it appears
on the websites of organizations that sponsor the popular writing contests.[232] What does that mean exactly? It's very hard
to pin down, but the idea is probably an attempt to burnish
the image of Islam in the U.S. as educated, charming Turkish
people explain their faith both here and abroad. As with many
other Muslims, Turks are all for inter-faith dialogue until they
believe they have the upper hand. Then, it becomes a one-way
conversation because, as Sultan Mehmet said, "there must be
only one religion," a bedrock Islamic doctrine.

"there must be only one religion."

229 http://www.taccenter.org/index.php?option=com_content&view=article&id=
     90&Itemid=292&lang=en (January 13, 2014).
230 http://www.clarionproject.org/analysis/turkey-stakes-claim-america-100-mil-
     lion-mega-mosque (October 13, 2013).
231 http://www.istanbulcenter.org/index.php?option=com_content&view=categor
     y&layout=blog&id=62& Itemid=61 (January 21, 2014).
232 Ibid.

I recently had a grandmother ask me if I thought that her granddaughter should fly to Istanbul after winning the essay contest in her region in Georgia. I said that they should think twice about letting a young lady who was not firmly established in her faith be subjected to a week's worth of propaganda regarding "moderate" Islam and "inter-faith dialogue." There's nothing wrong with going to Istanbul; it's a visually stunning city with a powerful allure. However, we should be careful that we are not unsuspecting naïfs who allow our children and grandchildren to be hosted by Turks for weeks at a time and fed a non-stop diet of the glories of Islam, as expressed in Turkey. Our children are a little too young to be able to separate fact from fiction and propaganda from a trip's "theme."

I'm not a full-blown conspiracy theorist and I don't think Turks are sitting in offices in Ankara saying, "Let's take over the world via essay contests." I do know, however, that Turkish leaders have often complained of Islamophobia worldwide, and they are happy to take the lead in recapturing a positive spin on Islam in the press and in the minds of the impressionable young. So, I have no doubt whatsoever that Turks in Ankara are at least saying, "Let's create a global campaign to present a palatable Islam that shows off our culture as well." They have that right, but we need to be discerning when we encounter that campaign.

From Tiger Woods hitting a golf ball across the Bosphorus,[233] and global sports icons Kobe Bryant and Lionel Messi serving as a lead spokespeople for Turkish Airlines (the largest airline in the world),[234] to Istanbul hosting the world basketball championships and making a strong bid for the 2020 Olympics, Turkey seems to be everywhere in the marketing universe.

---

233   http://www.businessinsider.com/heres-tiger-woods-hitting-a-golf-ball-from-europe-into-asia-2013-11 (January 21, 2014).

234   http://www.dailymail.co.uk/sport/football/article-2518114/Lionel-Messi-Kobe-Bryant-selfie-shootout-Turkish-Airlines.html (January 21, 2014).

ONE KEY NATION TO WATCH

It's a fascinating marketing juxtaposition to see Bryant and Messi photographing themselves in front of the Blue Mosque in Istanbul. Graphic designers would have a field day analyzing that curious mash-up of images. The impression people have of Turkey has gone from backward Muslims wearing the fez to modern nation on the move. And commercial spokespeople are not the only ones spreading Turkish influence. Arms salesmen are pulling in a haul of money too, as sales of weaponry grew an incredible 43 percent between 2008 and 2012.[235]

Tracking Turkey: Count the Headscarves

With its rapid rise, Turkey has had to weather several political storms as it evolves from a secular republic to a near-autocratic Islamic nation. Young, educated people who do not lean Islamist and did not vote for Erdoğan have taken to the streets in many cities to protest excessive governmental power and the probable death of a true democracy with liberal, secular values. These protests, the largest in many years in Turkey, showed the depth of anger against Erdoğan. One opposition party leader encapsulated the feelings about Erdoğan held by thousands who gathered across Turkey in 2013: "He thinks that he is empowered by God and that the only truth is what he thinks and what he says; he is intoxicated by power."[236]

In short, Mustafa Kemal Ataturk's vision of a secular Islamic republic fades with each passing year, as an openly Islamist government turns the screws tighter on a society that seemed to want to deny its Islamic heritage. Many times in Turkish streets, the locals would sigh as they told my wife and me that ten years ago almost none of the women wore headscarves, "and

235 http://www.hurriyetdailynews.com/turkeys-defense-exports-up-10-per-cent-to-14-billion.aspx?PageID=238&NID =60922&NewsCatID=345 (January 13, 2014).

236 http://www.washingtonpost.com/world/middle_east/turkish-protests-show-depth-of-anger-against-erdogan/2013/06/04/f9b8af42-cd22-11e2-9f1a-1a7cdee20287_story.html (June 5, 2013).

now, look!" We would be standing together looking at a sea of scarves in Istanbul, Ankara, and Konya – all around the country. Our secularized tour guides, fellow teachers, or students would always act ashamed by this supposed lack of freedom and religious backwardness. One of my French classes even did a video project in which they mocked the different styles available for headscarves, seeing it as a backward, primitive fashion accessory. I would always say, "Why are you surprised? You cannot keep Islam under wraps forever. You don't need to be embarrassed. It is what it is. This is who the majority of Turks are." That was no solace to another Turkish friend who recently visited with us and told us her opinion of a city in the East where she now teaches. What was her observation of this metropolis loaded with political conservatives and veiled women? "It's not my country. I hate it."

Couple the conservative fashion trends with the attempted blockage of YouTube and Twitter; the increasing restrictions on the sale of alcohol (banned from 10:00 p.m. to 6:00 a.m., health warnings on all bottles, no sales on airlines, etc.);[237] the ban of red lipstick for airline stewardesses (since overturned);[238] the reversal of a ban on headscarves in schools and government buildings;[239] the tweaking of university admissions policies to allow students from religious high schools to attend, even though many lack adequate academic preparation;[240] and, collectively, you can see the spread of Islamism almost by the day in Turkey.

I could write a book about the importance of headscarves in Turkey, but just believe me when I tell you that the wearing

---

237 http://www.reuters.com/article/2013/05/24/turkey-alcoholidUSL6N0E507H 20130524?feedType=RSS&feed Name=nonCyclicalConsumerGoodsSector& rpc=43 (May 25, 2013).

238 http://www.telegraph.co.uk/travel/travelnews/10048417/Turkish-Airlines-overturns-lipstick-ban.html (January 13, 2014).

239 http://www.bbc.co.uk/news/world-europe-24761548 (January 13, 2014).

240 http://nationalreview.com/article/348422/erdo%C4%9Fan%E2%80%99s-agenda#! (January 13, 2014).

of this small piece of fabric has far more emotional force attached to it than the American flag. You will never understand the place of the headscarf in Turkish society unless you are a Turk. Ataturk, the founder of the nation, banned them in public places in an attempt to modernize Turkey, believing that the best course for his nation was to imitate Europe in its sophistication and secularity. Ataturk also banned the popular fez, the Islamic caliphate in Istanbul, *sharia* courts, and several other leftovers from the Ottoman Empire.

You will never understand the place of the headscarf in Turkish society unless you are a Turk.

In stark contrast, Erdoğan has worked for years to overturn the ban on the scarves, saying, "We are ending prohibitions, oppression. No one can see themselves as the sole heir of the republic – those with headscarves are heirs as much as those who don't cover their heads." Critics saw the ban's overturn as just one more step towards Islamism, while supporters hailed it as an "overdue normalization in a country that is almost entirely Muslim."[241]

The best parallel I can think of to help you grasp the magnitude of this change is to imagine the Supreme Court ordering U.S. public schools to have Christian prayer reintroduced in them, as well as displays of the Ten Commandments. That would give you an idea of the religious weight that the headscarf carries in Turkey.

It's no wonder that nearly every day, Turkish columnists lament the slow death of their cherished secular society. As one recently wrote, "I think that the model or idea of post-Islamism has already started to crumble a very short time after it began its ascent."[242] Another even more famous writer painted the makeover under Erdoğan as "the struggle for Western lifestyles,

---

241 http://online.wsj.com/news/articles/SB10001424052702303442004579123320877810350 (October 10, 2013).

242 http://www.hurriyetdailynews.com/towards-the-end-of-post-islamism.aspx?pageID=449&nID=26090& NewsCatID=406 (September 14, 2013).

against an authoritarianism that imposes a conservative way of life ... The concept of the Muslim democrat has been suffocated ... While there was talk of a democratic Turkey as an example to other Muslim countries, we discovered an autocrat."[243] You can see such columns several times a week in Turkey's newspapers, and you wonder how long they will be allowed to speak out in this way, given the country's new title as "the world's biggest prison for journalists," according to Reporters Without Borders.[244] As the columnist quoted above added, "We need to underline that the Turkish press is no longer doing investigative reporting."[245]

Turkey's Multiple "Allies"

Erdoğan has pointedly led his country away from Europe and towards Islamist organizations in the Middle East. He is frequently photographed with leaders of the Muslim Brotherhood and Hamas. Also, during his reign, Turks' support for EU membership has plummeted from 75 percent to 44 percent, heeding their prime minister's reference to the organization being a "Christian club."[246] Before you assume that Turks are a Westernized ally of the U.S. who will never let us down, think about the fact that only a minority of Turks want to join the EU now, no matter how many jeans-wearing, longhaired, laid-back protestors you see on television waging a sit-in against the current government. That group is a sizeable one, but it is not the majority in Turkey. I often urge my readers not to be fooled by

243 http://www.hurriyetdailynews.com/this-is-the-struggle-for-the-survival-of-western-lifestyles-says-turkish-columnist.aspx?PageID=238&NID=60929&NewsCatID=338 (January 13, 2014).

244 http://nationalreview.com/article/348422/erdo%C4%9Fan%E2%80%99s-agenda#!.

245 http://www.hurriyetdailynews.com/this-is-the-struggle-for-the-survival-of-western-lifestyles-says-turkish-columnist.aspx?PageID=238&NID=60929&NewsCatID=338 (January 13, 2014).

246 http://www.huffingtonpost.com/david-l-phillips/european-union-leveragei_b_4435754.html?ncid= txtlnkusaolp00000592 (December 14, 2013).

the Western media's portrayal of a given country, as journalists seek out university-educated English speakers everywhere, concluding they are the power brokers, when in fact they are a small slice of the urban elite, not the heart and soul of a nation.

Turkey's drift from secular, West-leaning nation to Islamist, East-facing power is a fascinating evolution to witness. I can remember watching my students at a high school dance gyrating to the latest hip-hop song amidst smoke machines and strobe lights. I thought to myself, "When the revolution reaches its apex, these kids' heads will be the first to be chopped off." Many of their parents knew that, and I had several students tell me that their families were seriously considering emigrating within the next few years due to the changes in Turkey.

"When the revolution reaches its apex, these kids' heads will be the first to be chopped off."

Erdoğan's mandate to lead has been chipped away a bit as he faces continual backlash from the media which he has censored, the police departments which he has purged, and the military which he has neutered as he consolidates power in an amazing way. Turks ask me all the time what I think of him, and my answer is always: "He is a brilliant politician." Erdoğan has engineered a Putin-like grip on power, first changing the constitution to give the office of president more power, then running for president and winning decisively in August 2014, capturing more than 50 percent of the vote to avoid a runoff.[247] Thus, his twelve years in power will be extended by at least another term of five years, and probably two such terms. He is undoubtedly the most powerful politician in Turkey since Ataturk. That troubles many political observers. As one New York-based consultant told the *Wall Street Journal*, "The risk is that the whole system of checks-and-balance will be further weakened as he [Erdoğan] tries to experiment with this executive

---

247   http://online.wsj.com/articles/turks-cast-votes-in-presidential-election-with-
      erdogan-primed-for-win-1407658125 (August 11, 2014).

presidency, running state affairs from the palace and bringing everything to uncertain territory."[248]

The win also was Erdoğan's party's ninth straight in local and municipal elections over the past decade-plus. This followed his personal re-election triumph as prime minister in 2011, when his Justice and Development Party (AKP) romped to victory, with more than 50 percent of the vote nationwide, double the next closest party.[249]

Municipal elections in 2014 gave another clear referendum on how Turks feel about the AKP. As innumerable Western media speculated that Erdoğan's party would suffer setbacks and perhaps even lose control of Istanbul, the 90-percent turnout sent a clear message to those who cannot get rid of their ideas of Turkey as a moderate country. The percentage of voters who favored the AKP actually *rose* in 2014 as compared to 2009, from 39 percent to 45 percent.[250] Evidently, Turkish people do not mind a strongman at all.

One political commentator summed up the results this way:

> *Besides this clear victory for the AKP and Erdoğan, these elections bring us to three main conclusions. First of all, this victory is a kind of revenge for him against his opponents who have used his authoritarian policies and corruption scandals to attack him. … Secondly, it seems that Erdoğan's authoritarian policies and his harsh response to the popular unrest did not prevent him from winning this election. … Apparently, Turkish voters preferred a strong and capable leader, although authoritarian and corrupt, to other leaders that they consider unable to confront many challenges that Turkey faces.*[251]

---

248 Ibid.
249 http://www.theguardian.com/world/2011/jun/13/recep-erdogan-turkey-general-election (January 21, 2014).
250 http://carnegieendowment.org/2014/04/03/turkey-local-elections-gave-huge-victory-to-erdogan (August 8, 2014).
251 Ibid.

The "tyranny of the majority" is a tyranny nonetheless, and is "a vivid reminder that Turkey's democratic transition is both incomplete and subject to serious reversal," says a writer who has observed Turkey for many years. Future elections will give Turks the "chance to decide how much they care about an independent judiciary, a free press, and autonomous institutions," according to James Traub, a Fellow at the Center on International Cooperation and columnist for *Foreign Policy* magazine.[252]

The recent power grab in seeking to make the judiciary answerable to the prime minister's cabinet, not independent of it, is the latest red flag for the secularists. As long-time editor of one of Turkey's largest papers, Ertuğrul Özkök, stated recently:

> *If the government bill to give the administration more control over the judiciary is endorsed by the Parliament, let's state clearly that Turkey will be heading toward fascism ... We should not be slaves to Erdoğan ... When Islamists come to power, the moment they feel they are strong, the first thing they do is to impose their conservative values on everybody else ... I am 66 years old and I have seen a lot, yet I have never witnessed such an oppressive regime.*[253]

The Most Powerful Man That You Have Never Heard Of

Another fascinating aspect of Turkey's continued spread of its tentacles lies on a quiet farm in rural Pennsylvania, where Fethullah Gülen lives, one of *TIME* magazine's 100 "Most

---

252 *http://www.foreignpolicy.com/articles/2014/01/10/deja_vu_and_para-noia_in_the_deep_state_turkey_erdogan gulen#sthash.POxzY2Em.dpbs* (January 12, 2014).

253 *http://www.hurriyetdailynews.com/this-is-the-struggle-for-the-survival-of-western-lifestyles-says-turkish-columnist.aspx?PageID=238&NID=60929&NewsCatID=338.*

Important People" in 2013. This widely respected imam fled his homeland in 1999, ostensibly to seek medical treatment in the U.S. Most observers believe, however, that he was going to be arrested in Turkey for remarks he made in one speech calling for "nationwide restoration," so that Turkey would "be more fruitful on behalf of Islam," references to a possible plot to make Turkey an Islamic state. Despite his absence in Turkey, Gülen still has millions of acolytes in Turkey who carry out his agenda from afar, and with the billions that his organization has raised, they have founded more than 4,000 schools within Turkey, and another 500-plus in dozens of countries that mix academic excellence, English, and same-sex classes with Islamic teaching and an emphasis on service.[254] A total of 143 of those schools are in the U.S., and most people have no idea of the guiding philosophy that drives them, with names such as Magnolia Science Academy and Fulton Sunshine Academy.[255] By the way, Gülen and his followers talk a lot about "inter-faith dialogue" as well.

Gülen's network combines a fiercely nationalistic tone with a rigid observance of Islam, and until recently, had folded neatly into the AKP parade. That coalition has shown signs of fracturing in recent months, as Gülenite members of Parliament resign from the AKP and Erdoğan accuses Gülen of seeking to embarrass him through corruption probes that have exploded into the international media, powered by Gülen supporters in the military and police, according to conjecture.[256]

One of the strangest ironies of our time, I think, is that a smallish, elderly man living on a farm in rural Pennsylvania is deeply influencing the politics of one of the hottest nations in

---

254 http://news.yahoo.com/enigmatic-turkish-cleric-poses-challenge-erdogan-39-might-100631963.html (December 16, 2013).

255 http://turkishinvitations.weebly.com/list-of-us-schools.html (January 12, 2013).

256 http://news.yahoo.com/turkey-detains-ministers-39-sons-bribery-probe-160301629.html.

the world, while spreading a cheery and harmless Islam through an international web of schools, and this all under the nose of U.S. intelligence and the world media.[257] It's too far-fetched even to be a novel! I think Gülen is too old to be any kind of Antichrist figure, but I believe his wolf-in-sheep's-clothing brand of Islam is laying a perfect foundation for a seemingly harmless caliph in the near future. I do not doubt for a minute that we will look back at an Antichrist who fooled us all for a time, with his "Islam is tolerant" message urging "inter-faith dialogue," and realize that Gülen's web helped to prepare the world psychologically and spiritually for a slick Islamic takeover. We should all learn more about this man, and I would probably argue for the closing of his schools in the U.S., no matter how objective and harmless they seem to be. I don't consider myself unreasonably intolerant, but I also object to Islamism being pushed on American students under the guise of quality science and technology training. Here is a typical statement from his official website, which features a picture of what looks like a kind, gentle, elderly man:

> *I don't consider myself unreasonably intolerant, but I also object to Islamism being pushed on American students.*

> *Fethullah Gülen's understanding of duty, to serve humanity especially in the field of education, permits no expectation of material or political gain. Sincerity and purity of intention should never be harmed or contaminated. Fethullah Gülen's philosophy of education is not utilitarian, nor a social and political activity which can be divorced from the rest of his philosophy or faith, but a firmly integrated and well-developed component of his worldview. The purpose of the Gülen Movement is to*

---

257 http://online.wsj.com/news/articles/SB10001424052702304027204 5793 32670740491570?mg=reno64-wsj&url=http percent3A percent2F percent2Fonline.wsj.com percent2Farticle percent2FSB100014240527023 0402720457933267074049 1570.html&fpid=2,7,121,122,201,401,641,1009 (January 21, 2014).

*ensure respect for objective and universal human values,
to never have ulterior motives to seek material interests
nor to impose any ideology or to seize power through
politics in any country.*

*For over forty years, Fethullah Gülen has urged his
audiences to achieve the right balance of social justice
between the individual and community; to develop and
advance in every individual and the whole nation feelings of love, respect, altruism, striving for the sake of
others, sacrificing their own material and non-material
benefits and aspirations for the sake of others. There
has never been any evidence of an attempt by the Gülen
Movement to gain any kind of political power or material objectives in any of the regions where participants
work and volunteer.*[258]

Look for additional code words in this statement such as
"serve humanity," "universal human values," "social justice,"
"love," "respect," and "sacrificing." Who can argue against
such values and such an ideal? I hear echoes of the poetry of
Rumi, a Persian who lived in Turkey and is one of the most
popular poets in the world to this day.[259] He too spoke often of
love and preached a seemingly tolerant version of Islam, even
as he discipled whirling dervishes in Konya to make contact
with Allah through this mystical dance. Gülen reminds me of
Rumi, with his emphasis on love and service and the common
values of humanity. Those are all great emphases, but beware
the underside of Islam, which insists on its supremacy. The
Sufi branch of Islam, which Rumi championed, is a fascinating
study, especially as you learn the meaning behind the garments

---

258 *http://fgulen.com/en/gulen-movement/questions-and-answers/33592-are-the-
education-services-purely-altruistic-or-does-the-gulen-movement-have-other-
political-and-material-objectives-too* (January 21, 2014).

259 *http://www.rumi.org.uk/* (January 21, 2014) has a good sample of his poetry.

and dance of the whirling dervishes. Their elongated hats, for instance, are meant to symbolize death to self.[260] Disciples in this branch of Islam actually speak about a love for Allah, but they cannot invalidate the Koran, which always foresaw an entirely Islamic world. On the Whirling Dervishes website, you will see the same code words as you saw on Gülen's site, specifically "love," "tolerance," and "service." Who can argue against that?

Is Turkey Friend or Foe of the West?

The ability to charm people into a given school of thought is not uniquely Turkish, but the Turks have presented for decades an Islam that the West has more easily accepted. Think of how the Antichrist will be able to secure power in the world, form a peace agreement, and then break it midway through, as biblical prophecy seems to indicate. Add to this quality of charisma the geographical indicators that Scripture provides, and you can understand why more than a few Bible scholars are asking if Turkey will head up the ancient Antichrist alliance foretold in Ezekiel and other books. Even a few years ago, Turkey as part of some sort of powerful group in the End Times would have been laughable. The per capita income stood at $3,000; Turkey was considered a Third World nation; and no significant international events had taken place there in a hundred years, unless you count the Armenian Genocide.

Today, per capita income has tripled, cranes are ubiquitous, malls are being built everywhere, and the world marvels at yet another Turkish engineering feat. It would not be an exaggeration to call Istanbul one of the hottest cities in the world, with festivals and international competitions of all types being held there, as well as many hit movies being filmed there. Visitors

---

260 *http://www.whirlingdervishes.org/whirlingdervishes.htm* (January 21, 2014), a good site for details on Rumi's school of thought and these famous dancers.

to what may be the largest city in Europe now marvel at the new rail system tunneled under the Bosphorus Strait, and the floating parking decks in the water separating the European from Asian sides of Istanbul. The rail tunnel which connects Europe to Asia is the world's deepest and cost $4 billion, the type of project only a major developed country would even attempt. Dubbed the "Marmaray," as it runs under the Marmara Sea, the wonder has been "humbly" called "the project of the century" by the Turks.[261]

This book is not meant to serve as an exhaustive critique of U.S. foreign policy, but I think we would all do well to closely watch our country's relationship with Turkey. As Turkey turns more despotic and Islamic, it will inevitably move away from the U.S. as a long-time ally. As Paul Rubin, a scholar at the American Enterprise Institute, recently wrote:

> *The days of Turkey being 'a vital and strategic partner of the United States,' as Condoleezza Rice once described it, are over. A decade ago, Turks saw themselves as aligned with the United States, Europe and Israel; today Turkey is firmly in the camp led by Iran, Sudan, and Hamas. If Turkey is a bridge between West and East, it is now decidedly one-way.*[262]

Turkish attempts to supply Hamas terrorists, Erdoğan adviser links to al-Qaeda, and ambassador denials that al-Qaeda is a terrorist group are all troubling signs that indicate a move away from the U.S. and towards Islamism, Rubin added.[263] Spotty evidence that Turkey might even be supporting ISIS soldiers should also be thoroughly investigated.[264]

---

261 *http://www.bbc.co.uk/news/world-europe-24721779* (December 11, 2013).
262 *http://nationalreview.com/article/348422/erdo%C4%9Fan%E2%80%99s-agenda#!* (December 15, 2013).
263 Ibid.
264 *http://www.danielpipes.org/blog/2014/06/more-on-turkish-support-for-isis* (August 8, 2014).

Rubin lumped Turkey with Iran because evidence has surfaced that Turkey supplied Iran with $13 billion in gold in 2012-2013, in exchange for natural gas, flying in the face of international sanctions. Other evidence cited in a recent interview by a former terrorism finance expert with the U.S. Department of the Treasury points strongly to a very close relationship between Turkey and Hamas, a designated terrorist group, according to the U.S. government. Some Hamas leaders are based in Turkey, and the group receives $300 million *Many front companies funneling money to al-Qaeda are in Turkey.* from the Turkish government each year to build schools and mosques. Turkey also comes very close to being rated at the top of countries with international terrorist financial ties, just behind Iran and North Korea. Many front companies funneling money to al-Qaeda are in Turkey.[265] Do you group Turkey with Iran and North Korea in your mind as a member of the club of pariah states in the world? You probably should.

In view of its cooperation with openly Islamist groups and countries, Turkey's once-heralded relationship with Israel continues to deteriorate by the month. Political and military contacts, which used to be frequent, are now rare, with Erdoğan adding another brick in the wall by claiming he has evidence that Israel was behind the coup in Egypt that removed President Morsi from office. "The mood is so negative in the upper echelons of Turkey and Israel toward each other, it doesn't look like cooperation is possible," said Alon Liel, a former foreign ministry director general and diplomat to Turkey in the 1980s.[266] Most see the 2010 Israeli naval raid on a Turkish flotilla bound for Gaza as the flash point that poisoned the countries' relationship. Eight Turks and a Turkish-American were killed during

265 http://finance.yahoo.com/news/much-bigger-problems-turkey-could-133759643.html (January 13, 2014).
266 http://finance.yahoo.com/news/israel-turkey-relations-sink-low-140810502.html (October 10, 2013).

that raid. As someone who lived in Turkey during that time, I can tell you that the tape of those men being attacked and shot on those boats was replayed every single night for months as Turks called Israelis every name in the book and wondered aloud how the two countries had ever been friends. More than a few of my students said, "We are done with Israel," repeating what their parents said at the dinner table, parents who served in high places in the government and industry.

Does this sound like a country that the U.S. should continually praise and coddle? If you step back and forget what you've always thought about Turkey, you will see that this is a country calling Muslims around the world to assert their Islamism, not a West-leaning ally that longs to mimic the U.S. As Rubin said, those days are over. Yet, most observers agree that we cannot play too roughly with this long-time friend. As U.S. Treasury official Dr. Jonathan Schanzer said in an interview about raising the topic of Turkey's role in facilitating terrorism, "Yes, it will be a sensitive issue, and yes it will raise issues with Washington, but the alternative is unthinkable."[267]

That alternative would be labeling Turkey as a state sponsor of terrorism, a ghastly title for a supposed U.S. ally and member of NATO. "No one wants to do that, but the letter of the law is getting harder and harder to ignore that they might qualify," Schanzer added.[268]

Part of the point of this chapter is to have you understand that – the "unthinkable" is absolutely thinkable – as soon as the Islamic world gains enough stability, unity, and power to make Western friendships unnecessary and anti-Islamic. One truth that you learn very, very quickly in the non-Western world is how astute people and governments are about power. They will be very pragmatic in their relationships to gain power, and as

267 Ibid.
268 Ibid.

soon as they sense power increasing elsewhere, they will join that new bloc. I think this is absolutely what Turkey will do, having lived there and gotten to know Turkish Islam better. Turks have grudging respect for the U.S., but they do not consider us any sort of model for living. As soon as Muslim nations look even more hungrily to Ankara for leadership and they can become self-sufficient within the Islamic world, Turkey will ditch the EU and the U.S. faster than you can say "turquoise" – one of the few Turkish words to make it into English.

The longstanding ties between Turkey and the U.S., which include extensive military supply and planning, are also under siege. Turkey has begun a high-profile, public courtship of a Chinese anti-missile system, for example, a direct slap in the face to NATO and the U.S.[269] It is just one more bold move by Erdoğan and his team, who long for the day when the U.S. does not have to be assuaged. I will close this section with a quote from a nationalist poem used by Erdoğan in a famous speech that he gave when he was mayor of Istanbul, a speech that landed him in jail for four months in 1999 and banned him from political life in Turkey under the charge of "inciting hatred based on religious differences." That charge, and subsequent punishment, only raised his stature among devout Muslims in Turkey, helping to launch his later successful run for prime minister. Here is a look into the heart of this man that we make nice with constantly:

> Our minarets are our bayonets, our domes are our hel-
> mets, our mosques are our barracks. We will put a final
> end to ethnic segregation. No one can ever intimidate
> us. If the skies and the ground were to open against us.
> If floods and volcanoes were to burst, we will not turn

---

269 http://www.defenseone.com/politics/2013/10/congress-urges-hagel-us-
     block-turkey-china-anti-missile-deal/71831/?oref=d-interstitial-continue
     (January 13, 2014).

from our mission. My reference is Islam. If I am not able to speak of this, what is the use of living?[270]

Could an Islamist Turkey Produce the Antichrist?

This, my friends, is the core of Islamism, expressed in an emerging world power. So who cares? What difference does it make? I have watched the crystallization of thought among many prophetic writers in recent years, particularly those who foresee an Islamic Antichrist, as I do. It has been interesting to see a focus on Turkey from among these writers. I acknowledge wholeheartedly that Turkey could simply be the flavor of the month as we seek to locate the right Petri dish to produce the spirit of the Antichrist. I also confess to a deep fascination with this country, particularly after having lived there and studied the society up close and personal.

Looking back, if I can be a bit confessional here, I see that although my sojourn in Turkey was difficult (primarily due to loneliness and being packed into an expat community), I think God took me there to show me what was to come. I could not stop thinking about the type of person the Antichrist would have to be, the type of leader that most prophetic experts predict – slick, persuasive, able to bridge the Eastern and Western worlds in dress, manner, and understanding, and being well-spoken and fluent in English. It was not a great leap to imagine a Turkish man.

I remember my first day in class with my Turkish students. The adjective they chose again and again to describe themselves was "charming." I would tend to agree with that label, an interesting adjective to apply to the Antichrist too. Will he be a monstrous figure who repels people, or the kind of guy you think you could share a (non-alcoholic) drink with? I never

---

[270] *http://www.hurriyetdailynews.com/erdogan-goes-to-prison. aspx?pageID=438&n=erdogan-goes-to-prison-1999-03-27* (January 13, 2014).

thought the Antichrist would be someone dressed in Arab garb using broken English to persuade world leaders to go his way. I've always thought it would be a man who commanded respect, a man who knows where he is going, a man comfortable behind a microphone in a three-piece suit, yet possessing an Islamic faith that burns in his heart. Turks strike me as that sort of people, and I'm not alone in this thought.

Growing up, I always heard that Gog and Magog in biblical prophecy were Russia, reflecting the Cold War lenses that we used at the time to interpret Scripture. Now, lo and behold, we hear that Gog and Magog actually represent Turkey. This is part of the reason why I do not want to write a book focused strictly on interpretation of prophetic passages – I believe all of the interpretations that we come up with are colored by our biases. That said, the people who see Turkey as a possible cradle of the Antichrist spirit deserve a listen, I think. One truth I will write clearly for all of you to read is this: Turkey has ONE mindset, ONE perspective, ONE faith, and ZERO diversity. It is an incredibly patriotic and united place, and if you dig around a bit in people's souls, you stir up an Ottoman pride. My interactions with Turks have led me to pose this question to my audiences when I speak: "Guess who wants their empire back?"

Thus, with this caveat to beware of any interpretation of prophecy that gets too specific in a given age, let's take a brief look at the argument for a Turkish Antichrist. I have spent hours scouring literature and the Web to present the highlights of this perspective to you.

Here is what one prophecy scholar sees happening:

> Turkey is identified by multiple ancient place names/locations that existed within that country's current borders (i.e., Meshech, Tubal, Gomer, Togarmah). This

coalition of nations, and the Bible implies many more nations with them, will make an all-out assault on Israel, intending to destroy her. God told Ezekiel that this event would occur in the 'latter years' (Ezekiel 38:8). At the last moment it will look like Israel will be wiped out, but God will intervene and ... the other nations, including Iran, will suffer a 7-fold judgment from God – a great earthquake, pestilence, bloodshed, flooding rain, great hailstones, fire, and brimstone (Ezekiel 38:19-22). Finally, if the nations of the Middle East mentioned in Ezekiel 38 (i.e., Libya, Iran, Turkey, etc.) are right now coming into alignment with each other before our very eyes, and assuming that the incredible event described above occurs sometime during the Great Tribulation period as most Biblical scholars believe, how much closer are we then to the soon return of Jesus Christ?[271]

I think a restored Ottoman Empire is years away and will not have the same sort of structure that the former empire did. Sovereign governments are not going to simply yield to an arrogant Turkish sense of superiority. I could see, however, an Islamic bloc forming with a Turkish person as a savvy, English-speaking leader, familiar with the West and eager to lead the East's assertion.

Walid Shoebat, a former Palestinian member of the Muslim Brotherhood, has gained a wide hearing for his views on Islam's place in prophecy. He brings a fascinating point of view to a study of Scripture, noting in his public appearances that as he studied biblical prophecy, he felt as if he were reading an exact description of the Islamic messiah who is predicted to come, al-Mahdi, covered in the last chapter.[272]

---

271 *http://thelightseed.blogspot.com/2011_05_15_archive.html* (October 20, 2013).

272 *http://www.youtube.com/watch?v=SkPC2Sus_IU* (January 12, 2014) is an excellent example of Shoebat's teachings.

In a long article taken from his book *God's War on Terror*, Shoebat makes the following interesting points, some of which I think are very intriguing, others that might be considered a bit of a reach:[273]

- Ezekiel 38, one of the primary End Times passages in all the Word, "confirms Turkey's leadership role" due to five of the eight "nations" mentioned being located in Turkey.

- Revelation 17 re-affirms Turkey as the host of the Antichrist, with Istanbul as the empire that suffered a fatal wound but will return to stun the world. That blow, many would say, was the AD 1453 capture of the glorious city of Constantinople, a true wonder of the world that was taken over by the Turks. Now, Istanbul is one of the hottest cities in the world. Another interesting note is Istanbul has long been known as the "city on seven hills," which has a strange ring when you read this verse in Revelation 17: *The seven heads* [of the woman on the Beast] *are seven hills on which the woman sits. They are also seven kings. Five have fallen, one is, the other has not yet come; but when he does come, he must remain for a little while. The beast who once was, and now is not, is an eighth king. He belongs to the seven and is going to his destruction* (vv. 9-11).

- Daniel 9 says the Jewish Temple in Jerusalem will be destroyed by the *people of the prince to come* (v. 26). The unit of the Roman legion that leveled the Temple in AD 70 was based in Antioch in modern Turkey.

- Daniel 11 tells us of a "king of the North" who will be much like the Antichrist (an archetype of him). Most

---

273   *http://www.vriendenvanisrael.nl/?p=2155* (January 11, 2014).

prophecy scholars agree that this was Antiochus IV Epiphanes, the ruler of the Seleucid Division of the Greek Empire. Much of that king's reign was over modern-day Turkey.

- Isaiah's and Micah's frequent mentions of Assyria's opposition to Messiah Jesus further underscore the geographical proof of Turkey's role. The ancient kingdom of Assyria comprised much of modern Turkey.

- Zechariah 9 reaffirms Turkey's role as it says the sons of Zion will be roused against the sons of another kingdom. Verse 13 has often been translated as "sons of Greece," leading to many interpretations of the End Times centered around a revival of the Greek Empire, or the Western world as exemplified in Greek thought. But more careful, literal translations interpret this verse as "sons of Yavan." Who was Yavan? A grandson of Noah, whose descendants settled in western Turkey, many in the city of Izmir, a longtime biblical site. Another son of Yavan (or Javan) was Tarshish, now modern-day Tarsus, also in Turkey.

- The "throne of Satan" mentioned in Revelation 2 was constructed in Pergamum, a city whose spectacular ruins you can see in Turkey today, along with a reconstruction of that throne.

In addition to these seven "biblical proofs," Shoebat makes a powerful case for a Turkish Antichrist by noting that any Beast who would be able to dupe the nation of Israel into a peace treaty for three-and-a-half years would have to "have the reputation for being moderate and must possess the trust of the Israelis and the world." I agree. There will need to be some repair in the Turk-Israeli alliance before this can happen, but these two nations have shown a remarkable willingness to partner in hopes of keeping the rest of the Middle East calm, up until very recently. And despite the political tension between the two, the economic relationship remains strong, with a nearly 40 percent jump in trade reported in 2013.[274] Turkey and Israel have a history of cooperation, unlike Israel with other Middle Eastern neighbors. As long as Erdoğan is in power, I think this relationship will suffer, certainly if he continues to call Israel a "terrorist state."[275] However, the right person, someone with a smoother oratory, could certainly call on a shared history between the two countries and draw Israel to the negotiating table. Turkey is one of the few Middle Eastern countries that recognized Israel's right to exist immediately, on March 28, 1949. Bahrain, Iraq, Kuwait, Lebanon, Oman, Qatar, Saudi Arabia, Syria, the U.A.E., and Yemen still do not accept Israeli passports, and I don't see another country of consequence in the region that would be able to lure Israel into a peace treaty.

When searching for the Antichrist, one must never look to Ahmadinejads or Usamas of the world, but instead to someone with a moderate mask.

Shoebat affirms the common scriptural narrative that "the Antichrist will initially appear to be moderate and trustworthy, but he will also eventually show his true colors. And, his success will come through deceit and shrewdness." He added, "When searching for the Antichrist, one must never look to Ahmadinejads or Usamas of the world, but instead to someone with a moderate mask – at least in the beginning. His sinister, rabid hatred for Jews and Christians will not be revealed until he lures the sheep into his den."[276]

I could not agree more. Often when a fundamentalist leader jumps into the world spotlight, people ask if he is the Antichrist.

274 http://www.haaretz.com/business/.premium-1.603035 (January 21, 2014).
275 http://www.jpost.com/Diplomacy-and-Politics/Turkeys-Erdogan-calls-Israel-a-terrorist-state (January 21, 2014).
276 http://www.vriendenvanisrael.nl/?p=2155.

I don't think it will be that obvious to us. I think anyone able to pull off a peace treaty with Israel and then negotiate his way to global domination will look great, speak well in English, and be comfortable around all sorts of people from the West and East. I don't think he will wear Arab dress or be monolingual. I think he will look like a handsome politician and wear a variety of clothing to fit the context; he will be familiar with Western ways of thought, and he will probably have been educated at some point in Europe or the U.S. This fits the profile of many leaders in Turkey who have studied abroad and speak at least passable English. They present themselves and their country as moderate, tolerant, and inclusive, but they are not shy about their faith, either.

Is Turkey Tolerant and Open?

The idea that Turkey is tolerant to all is based partly on history, but is very difficult to pinpoint in reality today. I remember my students swearing that their country was diverse, tolerant, and inclusive. I would ask, "Well, then, where are the Jews in Turkey? The Armenians? The Christians?" They would tell me about a small neighborhood in Istanbul that was filled with Jewish people. I would reply, "One small neighborhood in a city of twenty million people. That is not diversity!" They did not argue with me too vociferously – rare for them.

The fact is the Turks have either killed or driven out all minority peoples and faiths. The Armenian Genocide in 1914-18 is increasingly recognized, even among Turks, as having occurred. One-and-a-half million Christians were expelled in 1923, and another 150,000 left after anti-Christian riots in Istanbul in 1955, helping to cut the Christian population from two million to a mere four thousand today.[277]

---

[277] http://www.aoiusa.org/blog/ecumenical-patriarch-bartholomew-i-feel-cruci-fied/ (January 15, 2014).

When you live in Turkey, these figures are not just numbers; they show in living proof every day you walk the streets. One of the most difficult aspects of residing in Turkey was seeing the same sort of people with the same hair color, same language, same speech pattern, same facial features, and same mindset every single day. Turkey was the absolute antithesis of "diverse." That's why it is 99-plus percent Islamic and extremely united as a country. It also has a fairly low crime rate, which is true of all homogeneous countries. Despite its thriving tourism and claim to welcome all nationalities, Turkey is far, far less diverse than Egypt, Lebanon, or even Libya. Even though it has long been considered a friend to America and has a NATO membership, Turkey is as Islamic in composition as Iran. Does Iran seem diverse and "open" to you? Turkey is just as closed psychologically and ethnically, behind the charm, the student exchanges, and the warm welcome of foreign teachers, including me. I would also add that it was the hardest place I've lived in to learn the language. Classes were available, but Turks on the street were not helpful at all. Some asked, "Why are you learning Turkish?" while others insisted it was too hard for Americans to learn. I think Turks enjoyed keeping their secrets to themselves, and the longer I lived there and the deeper I dug into the society by persistent questioning of friends, the uglier it became. That happens everywhere, I think, but Turks like to present a front of impeccable morality, joy, and good humor. They fear foreign influence and a distillation of their patriotic passion. They certainly never seemed to want to help me learn Turkish.

Whenever I share this perspective with fellow Americans who have been to Turkey, they always say, "But I found them to be so polite, so helpful." Turkish people *are* very charming, as I've said, and they can be amazingly relational when they want to sell you something or when you are a tourist. As a good friend of mine in Turkey said when I was there, "There's a big difference between arriving in a village for a few days – and saying that you will be moving in there." He was dead right. The initial hospitality turns to suspicion and distrust. Just because a person is warm and gracious upon first encounter does not mean that he or she does not harbor all sorts of racist and bigoted notions. I will share this story about the supposed tolerance of Turkey; it will explain a lot:

> As my wife and I arrived on the grounds of the university where we would be teaching in the prep school in Ankara, we noticed a stunning, modern mosque built right at the school's entrance, a truly breathtaking structure. We marveled at the architecture and were told that, in the spirit of the mosque's builder and the university's founder (Harvard-educated, by the way), there was even a room set apart on the picturesque grounds for Christians to use, if requested.

> I made a mental note of this promise and asked the next Easter if the cell group I had started would be able to use the room for a special worship service. I approached the taciturn school secretary who I was told could make anything happen on campus. She told me to write a letter and send it to her, documenting the request, and she would send it on to the proper authorities, whom she called "Building and Grounds Staff."

> I assumed the use of the room would be a shoo-in if maintenance staff were the only ones involved in authorizing our usage. After waiting several days, I went back to the secretary and she told me that there was no news. This process was repeated once a week for at least a month. My suspicions about Turkish tolerance were beginning to resurface. Finally, a few days before Easter,

*the powerful secretary showed her cards. She informed
me: "Authorization for that room has not been approved
yet." That sounded like something that came from higher
up than a custodian! I wondered what the decision
makers thought a group of twenty-five Christians would
do on Easter morning. Light fire to the mosque? Start a
spiritual revolution on campus?*

*I asked the secretary a few more times after Easter
if authorization had been approved, and she would
instantly tell me, "No." I eventually gave up.*

This story is classical Turkish "tolerance." On the surface,
it looks as if religious minorities will be welcomed to practice
their faith as they see fit. Upon further inspection, however,
Christians were not allowed to meet in the room designated
for them in a religious complex. The promise was, in fact, a lie.
Perhaps this is why the Ecumenical Patriarch of the Orthodox
Christian Church, Bartholomew, told *60 Minutes*, "I feel crucified" living under a Turkish government that "would like to see
his nearly 2,000-year-old Patriarchate die out," as the church's
seminary was shut down and part of its property seized, like a
python slowly squeezing a victim to death.[278]

Turks continue to fight the notion that they are xenophobic and
rigidly Islamic, whether that be through various "cooperation"
societies or the rhetoric of Gülen. As the idea that Turkey could
be the home of the Antichrist has gained circulation, Turkish
imams are fighting back even as they agree to be interviewed
by American authors such as Joel Richardson. To get a visual
idea of how Turkey sees itself and how religious teachers there
respond to the idea that their country could produce someone as
hated and feared as the Antichrist, I would recommend watching any number of YouTube videos showing the follow-up to

---

278 Ibid.

interviews between Richardson and Adnan Oktar, a renowned Islamic teacher who oversees a popular website bursting with information on al-Mahdi. In a soft, calm, reasoning voice, Oktar says that labeling Turkey as the Antichrist "makes the slaying of the Muslim world lawful," and then asks where the "love" is that he expects to see in Christians. He also derides the Christian idea that someone seeking world peace could possibly be an Antichrist, including this statement: "All Muslims are affectionate and compassionate." It's a fairly brilliant turn of the argument on its head as he shows clear contempt for Richardson's theory that the Antichrist will arise from Turkey, differentiating clearly between the Turkish brand of Islam and al-Qaeda. Among his last statements in part 1 of his series was:

> It is wrong and illogical to portray Turkey as the
> Antichrist. It is cruelty ... You fail to think the best
> ... You must trust people ... You are sowing the seeds
> of hatred in all Christians' hearts ... You should be
> demanding warmth and brotherhood ... We believe in
> the same Allah, don't we?[279]

I have interacted a lot with Richardson, who has written several books on the topic, including *Mideast Beast: The Scriptural Case for an Islamic Antichrist* and *God's War on Terror: Islam, Prophecy and the Bible*, and I enjoyed corresponding with him as I did the final edits on my first book. I can assure you that he loves Muslims, but he is not shy about sharing his ideas regarding where Islam is headed. In that respect, we are alike.

Oktar's angle that Christians claiming the Antichrist will be a Muslim are bigoted and hateful can give you an idea of why this book had to be examined by several publishers before it was printed. This theory can be construed as hateful, but the irony is that it springs from the minds and hearts of people

---

279 *http://www.youtube.com/watch?v=znhACywX_IQ* (January 14, 2014).

who have spent years among Muslims, and love them enough to tell the truth.

Just by watching Oktar on video, you will get an idea of the Turkish take on Islam, and you will hear all of the code words I've mentioned in this chapter, including "love" and "peace." Who is against those? You might have a very hard time picturing someone like Oktar carrying a sword, but I would submit that the Turkish expression of Islam that I witnessed with my own eyes is the perfect manifestation of Islam for an Antichrist figure to adopt: a winsome Islam, if you will, backed by a legendary toughness on the battlefield. Turks are known the world over for their grit in warfare, from their post-World War I defense of Anatolia to their role in the Korean War.[280]

Turkey merits our most careful attention in the years to come.

For the many reasons I've stated in this chapter – from Turkey being the site of the largest Muslim empire in the world and the only country seeking to revive such an empire, to possible scriptural evidence for the "Lost Land of the Bible" being a key country in the End Times – I believe Turkey merits our most careful attention in the years to come. As I lived in Turkey, I found a brand of Islam that I think would play very well in the modern world as a deceptive lure into the religion of Muhammad. There is just enough charm, Sufi-inspired emotion, and emphasis on "love," "understanding," and "tolerance" to make a Turk a prime candidate for the Antichrist, someone who appears quite palatable with politically correct people, yet who has a burning desire to spread Islam across the globe.

I will close this chapter with a famous Turkish saying that I learned from one of my students: "Slap me nine times, I do nothing. Slap me ten times, I will kill you."

Could this be the mantra for an Islamic Antichrist, a man

---

280 *http://archive.worldhistoria.com/turkish-soldiers-in-the-korean-war_topic9671_page2.html* (January 14, 2014).

who tolerates violations of the peace pact that he initiates, saying that he tried very hard to remain tolerant and loving, yet now is forced to invade, destroy, and behead? I think the chances of this figure coming from ancient Anatolia are great.

The first five chapters of this book have painted a fairly gloomy outlook, and I'm sorry for that. I am, by nature, a fairly optimistic individual. Yet I feel compelled to warn of a tsunami I've seen building abroad, a wave that has no sign of abating, but has actually grown in size and destructive power since the cataclysmic events of the Arab Spring.

So how should we respond to all of this? What can we learn from our brothers and sisters who are living a Matthew 24 life right now in Syria, Egypt, Libya, and Tunisia? I have a few thoughts to share in chapter 6.

CHAPTER SIX

What We Need to Do to Prepare

Granted, the rule of the world by an Islamic Antichrist is many years away, if it happens at all. Unreached people groups wait to be effectively penetrated with the gospel, although their number is far smaller than many think. The Islamic world needs to gain strength, unity, and leverage in order to face down the West. God continues to delay the return of Christ because He wants all people to come to repentance, as Scripture clearly tells us in 2 Peter 3:9. It will be several years before the Church in America experiences true persecution, beyond Christian television stars being temporarily suspended from their shows and Democrats being elected president, if you count those sorts of incidents as persecution. Many of my conservative friends do, judging from their Facebook posts.

These sorts of invented persecutions, coupled with the banning of school prayer and nativity scenes in public, two other logical moves by a government that doesn't want to be seen favoring one faith over another (which, by the way, was another idea of our founding fathers, a fact people conveniently skip over), pale in comparison to the Matthew 24 reality many of our brothers and sisters face in Arab Spring countries and elsewhere in the Middle East.

I think sometimes we feel subconsciously guilty in the West about not facing any sort of tangible persecution, after years of hearing testimonies of pastors being jailed in China, Christians being beaten in India, and Coptic believers being murdered while their churches burn to ashes. We want to join the club and say, "We're persecuted too!" Not really, nothing like what others face, and we should thank God for that every day, rather than invent some sort of minor prohibition of openly Christian practice in a pluralistic country.[281]

Rather than try to play the persecution card, let's look at how Christians experiencing true crucibles are reacting in real time to Great Tribulation-like persecution. Let's begin in Egypt, since it has received the most press coverage for the response of its historic Christian community to a lawless persecution by Islamists enraged by everything from a military coup ousting President Morsi, to a sense that with power given to the people, Egypt could finally become completely Islamic.

The primary responses we see in Arab Spring countries, some of which Jesus endorsed, include:

1. Running from the persecutors

2. Remaining on site and taking up arms

3. Remaining on site and insisting on legal protection

4. Yielding to persecutors while actively ministering to them

I have documented option 1, which has occurred in several Middle Eastern countries over the past decade and threatens the extinction of Christianity in that region of the world, a fact that even prominent government leaders are beginning to acknowledge.[282]

Option 2 has gained little headway, despite a call from Greek Orthodox Bishop Lukas al-Khoury in Syria to have Christians take up arms "to protect Syria, churches, and convents."[283] Some

---

281 See this article for an outstanding summary of this phenomenon: *http://www.relevantmagazine.com/god/church/myth-persecuted-american-church* (December 30, 2013).

282 *http://www.telegraph.co.uk/news/politics/10450617/Christians-face-extinction-amid-sectarian-terror-minister-warns.html* (December 20, 2013).

283 *http://www.news.va/en/news/asiasyria-archbishop-hindo-inciting-christians-to-* (December 26, 2013).

WHAT WE NEED TO DO TO PREPARE

believers undoubtedly have, but the loudest voices have decried this exhortation, saying that it violates the spirit of Christianity. Syrian Catholic Archbishop Jacques Behnan Hindo responded to the call to arms in this way: "As men of the Church, we cannot incite Christians to take up arms and to take part in the conflict. We cannot say these things; it is insane. It goes against the gospel and Christian doctrine."[284] In my research, I have not come across any reports that indicate Syrian Christians are standing and being resistant militarily to Islamist attacks.

Given the love of guns in many parts of America and the independent-militia thinking I've heard in certain Christian circles, many of whom contemplated rebellion upon the election of Barack Obama, I can foresee some U.S. pastors urging their congregations to "stand their ground." I recently had dinner with a pastor who delightedly told me of his church offering shooting classes as part of their women's ministry. A man like him would be first to urge application of his church's training when Muslims knock on doors and demand conversion.

That's why I'm writing this chapter, so we can all think through *how we should react* when the Great Tribulation comes.

Archbishop Hindo, in Syria, wisely added this comment when reacting to the call to arms: "The situation in which we find ourselves, every individual, even Christian, is free to make his own choices according to conscience."[285] That gives some wiggle room for Christian militias, but I would lean towards the no-armed-resistance stance. Taking up arms could make Syrian Christians even more of a target in that country, some have noted, and if we fight gun for gun, we don't present any sort of contrast to the typical Islamic ideas of "might makes right" and revenge is obligatory to protect one's honor.

---

284 Ibid.
285 Ibid.

Did Jesus Advocate Running?

Jesus certainly didn't seem to condone option 2 as He spoke in Matthew 24. Actually, it sounds as if He recommended option 1, although in other passages involving persecution, He seemed to argue for option 4. As a reminder, here are His exact words in verses 16-20:

> *Then let those who are in Judea flee to the mountains. Let no one on the housetop go down to take anything out of the house. Let no one in the field go back to get their cloak. How dreadful it will be in those days for pregnant women and nursing mothers! Pray that your flight will not take place in winter or on the Sabbath.*

Christ seems to favor option 1 and never encourages a running *towards* martyrdom. Paul, too, never seemed to advocate seeking to be killed for Christ's sake. Rather, he fled several times when he knew that his life was threatened, twice within the space of a few verses in Acts 9 (Acts 9:25, 30; 14:6, 17:10)! We know of Paul purposefully leaving at least four towns because of threats to his life. If you count other places where he left soon after starting an uproar, that number could climb to near ten. Don't let anyone tell you that Paul never ran. He did! Self-preservation, the most basic human instinct, seems to be compatible with sold-out Christian living. I think we can make a very strong biblical case for running in the midst of persecution. In a similar way, I do not see convincing biblical evidence for having a death wish and actively seeking martyrdom, something Muslims do to "guarantee" a place in paradise.

Christ never encourages a running towards martyrdom.

God does not call us to be cowardly, but Christ Himself advocated flight, and Paul lived out that commandment many times in his ministry. Remember these truths when the heat turns up and someone near you is insisting that God wants everyone to stand and fight, be outgunned, and go down in a blaze of glory. Once you are gone from this earth, you are gone, and you won't be able to win anyone else to Christ. You also might leave your family heartbroken and in great need. We need to be careful that we don't adopt a martyr complex, as Muslims have heartily done around the world.

Do Muslims Want Christians to Fight Back?

Some church leaders in Egypt believe that Muslims have actually wanted Christians to pursue option 2 and take up arms. Reverend Khalil Fawzi, pastor of the largest evangelical congregation in the Middle East, Kasr El Dobara Evangelical Church, said recently that Muslim Brotherhood supporters in Egypt want to begin a civil war and would be helped in their quest by Christians turning violent. "They hoped the Christians will retaliate by killing and a civil war would start. I praise Christians for their patriotic attitude."[286]

What will "patriotic" look like in the U.S.? I doubt it will look exactly like what plays out in Egypt. I also know from a decent understanding of war, and especially civil wars, that a lot of killing can be justified when the aggressors claim their murdering occurred in "war-like" conditions. (Turkey's defense of its mass killing of Armenians in the early twentieth century is a prime example.) So if we do stand and fire, Muslims will have an easy out for killing men, women, and children who would otherwise be innocent bystanders. That's why we need to think through organizing militias – it could set the stage for even more widespread slaughter. Your selfish act of grabbing an armload of guns could lead to your entire town being leveled. Is it worth that? I think Egyptian believers realize that fighting back with arms will only further endanger their brothers and

---

286 http://www.washingtontimes.com/news/2013/aug/20/egypts-coptic-christians-face-unprecedented-repris/#ixzz2ocRINmCk (December 26, 2013).

sisters in the faith. We need to carefully track their reaction as they live out Matthew 24 right now.

We can learn much from our brothers and sisters in the Middle East who have selected options 3 and 4. Let's take a closer look at lessons for us as we prepare for future peril.

Here are the primary lessons I see from Christians being persecuted by Muslims as I write:

1. They understand once and for all that the church is not a building.

Two days after the famed Archangel Michael Church was destroyed in Cairo, Coptic Orthodox Pope Tawadros II reminded his flock of what Jesus preached: "If the hands of evil kill, destroy and torch, then God's hands are greater and they build. Christ's commandments to us are love your enemy, bless those who curse you, and do good to those who abuse you."[287]

The reaction to this charge, and other similar exhortations, has been Christians calmly meeting for worship in the areas of their churches that have not been completely burned to the ground, as seen in the *60 Minutes* segment on Coptic Christians. The moving sight of Christians sitting in a room with one wall missing and the smell of burned wood still lingering, worshipping Jesus in a simple service, speaks volumes about understanding that the church is not a building.[288]

Tweets from Egyptian Christians after dozens of their meeting places were destroyed succinctly stated what we have always known about where the church is: "Churches are not just bricks and mortar. They are in our hearts."[289]

---

287 *http://www.miamiherald.com/incoming/article1957487.html* (November 22, 2013).

288 *http://www.cbsnews.com/videos/the-coptic-christians-of-egypt/* (December 15, 2013). You can watch the entire segment at this site.

289 *http://midnightwatcher.wordpress.com/2013/08/29/egypt-despite-losing-churches-homes-an-businesses-christians-refuse-to-react-to-islamist-provocations/* (December 30, 2013).

I think many Americans have come to realize this truth, as small groups have gained popularity over the past twenty years or so. That is a good realization to hold onto, because we could very well come to a time when we are not allowed to meet in buildings.

I was struck by this possibility as I toured a literal underground church in Turkey's Cappadocia region, mentioned in Acts 2:9 and 1 Peter 1:1. Our Muslim tour guide took us down a hole through which the four members of my family could barely squeeze. We walked among intricate hallways carved from stone, were told where meals were prepared and where people slept. It was an incredible experience to imagine living under the earth with brothers and sisters in Christ as we walked in the cool, moist tunnels, trying to imagine how we would fare in such conditions. Our guide was reluctant to tell us when the underground city was dug out of stone, but we later learned that it was used to escape Muslim raiders in the seventh century. History will repeat itself, I believe, and we will be meeting somewhere in secret to worship Jesus. I'm not arguing for a hardcore survivalist plan, but I am asking you to imagine meeting in a small group away from public sight. Where would that be in your community?

I also got a taste of this in West Africa when I ran a seekers' Bible study for Muslims who were considering the truth of the gospel. We met fairly openly in a neighbor's courtyard (got rained out once in three years!), but we did have to meet after the sun went down, so those who came could not be publicly identified. It was a lot of fun meeting under the cover of darkness, drinking mint tea until midnight and discussing the things of God. It was the best small group I'd ever been in, and I think we might have the chance to host similar groups one day.

Another group that met at night exclusively was the Protestants in Paris during the centuries of religious wars in France, with the Catholics often gaining the upper hand, particularly in the sixteenth century. I will never forget a friend acting as tour guide as he showed us where the man responsible for translating the Bible into French had lived, and how the Protestants were called the "Werewolves of Paris" because they only met at night. If you want to study persecution in Western contexts, French history could provide you with plenty of painful material, by the way.

Again, where would your meeting place at night be? Where would the "Werewolves" of your city, town, or neighborhood meet?

Other travels that have made me reflect on this style of church life included a visit to Antioch in Turkey. As we walked into the small cave where worship was held, a fairly underwhelming site despite the huge wall the Crusaders built outside it centuries ago, we saw escape routes carved into the stone, where church members probably fled Roman authorities. To see these passageways with your own eyes reminds you of where Christianity has been in the past, how it has been practiced, and how it will be practiced again, I think. The cave churches throughout Cappadocia (above ground) provoke similar thoughts. Church buildings did not come until much later in Christianity's development, probably in the fourth century.[290] Returning to a no-frills practice of following Jesus will be good for all of us. We will remember what our faith is all about, and there will be no more arguments over the color and style of the carpet in the sanctuary!

Returning to a no-frills practice of following Jesus will be good for all of us.

An exciting training development, one which could help us prepare for building-less Christianity, has gained great popularity in the body of Christ over the past several years

---

290 *http://www.christianitytoday.com/ch/asktheexpert/ask_churchbuildings.html* (January 2, 2014).

by readying people for possible service on the mission field, particularly among Muslims. TOAG, or "Training Ordinary Apprentices to Go," seeks to teach people to "do church" in small group settings, away from large worship gatherings that will not be available abroad.[291]

Participants spend ten months learning how to reach unreached peoples and develop authentic community in a small group setting. Families with children are welcomed in, and future workers for Christ are being much better prepared than earlier generations of believers. I've heard from a few that have participated in TOAG that it is difficult, yet rewarding. The method's founders state well the goal of the training:

> During TOAG, interns learn to be a Kingdom Community without including Western structures that often hinder movements. They experience life-in-community with other interns, something more akin to the Book of Acts. By taking a short sabbatical from present ecclesiastical structures, which include powerful (& professional) music, well crafted homilies (by highly trained professionals) in safe, comfortable surroundings (expensive buildings), interns experience first-hand what is and is not required for believers to be a 'Kingdom-Community,' experimenting with simple, organic structures capable of sharing the life changing power of God's Kingdom and reproducing into movements. ... These are just some of the reasons why many Americans benefit from the hands-on learning experience of TOAG.[292]

When I started a small group in Turkey for expat Christians and interested Turks, I didn't know about TOAG and didn't call my group any such name. It was a near-necessity, however, because the only church anywhere near my apartment was

291   For information on this radical training, look here: *http://toag.net/*.
292   Ibid.

ninety minutes and two bus rides away. Rather than make that trip and hope that other believers joined me, I started a small group in people's apartments. We had a rich time of sharing over the next eighteen months, forming our own mini-church, and building community as best we could.

What does all of this mean for you? Well, if you are what many call a "consumer Christian" and have chosen a church based on what it could provide for you and your family, then you are going to be in big trouble when the church in America is boiled down to the essentials. There will be no more album-worthy praise music concerts on Sunday morning, no more gigantic children's or youth programs held in state-of-the-art facilities, no more sermons broadcast via satellite of the mega-church's founding pastor.

No, it's going to be you, your family, a few other families (whom you may or may not like), and a few Bibles. Are you ready? Does this sound appealing? Begin to develop the type of Christian life that doesn't need a large church to sustain it and a walk with Jesus that values true community, not backseat participation – in effect, non-participation. You might grow as never before under persecution, as millions around the world can testify, and as Paul testified clearly in Romans 5:3-5:

> We also glory in our sufferings, because we know that suffering produces perseverance; perseverance, character; and character, hope. And hope does not put us to shame, because God's love has been poured out into our hearts through the Holy Spirit, who has been given to us.

In other words, we will experience hope in a new way as we are persecuted, as our focus will quickly turn to the world to come. Suffering will purify us of our preoccupation with the current material world. God will grow us all up in a hurry under such conditions, and those of us who have long lamented the differences between the church of Acts and the modern church will get a chance to see many of those differences wiped away in an instant. It will be an exciting time – American Christians finally able to live like the church of Acts! We have longed for this; we have prayed for this. Suffering under Islamic persecution will make it a reality.

2. Middle Eastern Christians have learned what it means to bless those who persecute them, but also to insist on justice where possible.

Christians in Syria are learning daily how to do this as I write. Many have chosen to stay in their towns and cities, even if Islamist rebels have overrun them and raped, looted, tortured, and killed them. As Open Doors USA spokesperson Emily Fuentes has reported, based on eyewitness accounts:

> There are some Christians who are fleeing because they have no other choice, but there are many Christians who have really felt God's call to stay in town, even though they have been attacked and targeted because of their faith. They realize that God's using them, and (are reaching) out to their Muslim neighbors.[293]

This is occurring despite the fact that Christians are being attacked specifically because of their faith, not just because they are getting caught in a crossfire of violence as the battle continues. Fuentes added: "There has been looting, physical attacks, there has been kidnapping and just a bunch of difficult and horrific things; parts of town being bombed and attacked because they are Christian."[294]

In Egypt, where more than forty churches were destroyed in the months following former President Morsi's removal from

---

293 http://www.christianpost.com/news/persecuted-syrian-christians-stay-ing-behind-reaching-out-to-muslim-neighbors-despite-attacks-106000/ (November 20, 2013).

294 Ibid.

office via a military coup in July 2013, Christians who had not fled the country continued to calmly meet for worship and show forgiveness to Muslims who broke the steeples of their churches as they screamed, "Allah is great!"[295] As one church's caretaker said, sitting in front of a devastated church building, "Whatever they couldn't carry, they destroyed." Believers met while sitting in front of a wall with graffiti proclaiming "Egypt is Islamic!"

Can you put yourself in that setting? Sitting in your church with the back wall blown out, as graffiti on the wall where worship banners used to hang reads, in plain English, "America is Islamic!" Close your eyes and picture that for a moment. What would you feel? Then, say a prayer for your brothers and sisters in Egypt who are living this *right now*.

The real moment when the Copts learned that "they were on their own; no one was going to help them," as Bob Simon reported on *60 Minutes*, was when they looked at the ruins of their churches – paintings ruined, Bibles burned, pews stolen – and understood their perceived support of the military coup to oust Morsi meant they were fair game for Islamists all over the country.

"Suffering, Copts believe, deepens their faith," Simon reported. "We were surprised that there was no anger, no call for revenge," he added, after attending a worship service in the one room not burned to the ground in one church. He explored this concept with Bishop Thomas, a Copt leader, who replied, "Forgiveness is a very important principle of the Christian life. When you are able to present forgiveness and love, you are able as well to ask for justice. One day in this life, justice has to be fulfilled."[296]

In other words, Copts are willing to die for their faith, but they also will continue to insist on constitutional protection of their people, as any Christian should. When Jesus said "turn

---

295 *http://www.cbsnews.com/videos/the-coptic-christians-of-egypt/* (December 8, 2013).
296 Ibid.

the other cheek," He said it in a society that guaranteed no rights for His followers. If we live in a country that does protect those rights, we should insist on them for as long as the legal code covers us, which it probably will in the early days of the Great Tribulation.

In other parts of Egypt, church leaders continue to insist on some sort of protection from the government, although little has been given. I don't see anything wrong with insistence on one's rights in this context. As Anba Makarios, the Orthodox Bishop of Minya in northern Egypt where a church was destroyed, said, "We strongly reject any attempt to involve the Church in the quarrels some are having with the security agencies, and we fully appreciate the efforts the Ministry of the Interior is making to enforce law and order."[297]

We will have the basic option of running, or remaining and seeking to win our attackers and fellow refugees to Christ.

Thus, it seems to me that we will have the basic option of running, or remaining and seeking to win our attackers and fellow refugees to Christ. The choice that we make will be a matter of conscience, as Scripture can be used to support both. Believers in both Syria and Egypt have made different choices.

I know that it can be very, very difficult for us to show grace to other Christians who choose differently than we do in matters that are not spelled out clearly in the Bible. We American Christians have a horrible time showing grace to members of another political party, parents who send their children to public schools, believers who don't speak in tongues or do speak in tongues. We really struggle with unity, if we are honest. Our individualistic culture, which holds the rugged, loner cowboy as an icon, does not breed Christian harmony. We do not have a sterling track record of graciously allowing

---

297 http://midnightwatcher.wordpress.com/2013/08/29/egypt-despite-losing-churches-homes-an-businesses-christians-refuse-to-react-to-islamist-provocations/.

differences of opinion in the body of Christ, as our 35,000 non-denominational churches attest.[298]

In conditions of intense persecution, I think options 1, 3, and 4 are all valid – running, staying and insisting on rights, and staying to minister and forgive. Are you prepared to show grace and love to your brother who flees? Are you prepared to show grace to your sister who stays? Get ready for that very real possibility of your church going its separate ways as people make different choices as Islamic law is applied in the U.S.

3. Churches have become de facto refugee care centers in the Middle East, not houses of worship alone.

In the parts of Syria where church buildings have not been desecrated, they have become de facto relief agencies, providing clothes, food, and Christian teaching. These churches are seeing people come to faith in Christ as the congregants love everyone who has been made homeless, not just Christians. This is in stark contrast to the Islamic approach to provide aid for Muslims only. Among those who have come to faith has been at least one diehard Islamist.[299]

As Syrian Christians have ministered to all people as war rips their country apart, they ask not for relief from the persecution, for money, or any sort of assistance, but primarily for prayer. Syrian Christians know prayer is the only way that peace will come to their country.[300]

What an amazing witness, to care for everyone in the midst of intense suffering. The Church has done this throughout history. I would venture to say all of the books in the world's libraries would not be enough to tell the stories of instances when Christians helped people in desperate need, regardless of

298 *http://hirr.hartsem.edu/research/fastfacts/fast_facts.html* (December 30, 2013).
299 *www.christianpost.com/news/persecuted-syrian-christians-staying-behind-reaching-out-to-muslim-neighbors-despite-attacks-106000.*
300 Ibid.

skin color or creed. I think of the immense reaction in the U.S. whenever a natural disaster occurs, such as Hurricane Katrina or the annual tornadoes in the Midwest.

We don't give ourselves enough credit as a national body of Christ-followers in this area. Many times I will say to my wife when I see an outpouring of this sort of charity, "Only in America," and it's true. I think we will get many more chances to show this unique, blind love, and we'll see diehard atheists, and other secularists, come to Jesus as we save their lives, at least temporarily, on this planet. It will be an exciting time of harvest.

One experience I had abroad in helping Muslims amidst incredible suffering was after the great market fire in my city of Bouaké, West Africa. The immense marketplace served a population of one million with its acres and acres of wooden stalls manned primarily by Muslim traders. The secular government, which was considered "Christian" by Muslims in the northern part of Côte d'Ivoire, insisted that the traders move next door to a concrete, government-built market at more than twice the rental cost.

When the Muslim traders refused to budge, a fire was mysteriously lit in the four corners of the market. A few hours later, it was burned to the ground, with many men jumping into the flames, knowing their businesses were ruined and they could never pay the debts they owed. Many of those traders had buried their life savings in the ground behind their counters in their market stall areas; when the market burned, so did their nest egg.

Thousands of others fled for Mali and Burkina Faso in the days that followed, seeking to escape debt and a very hostile work environment. The church planting team I was on decided to ask American supporters for funds to help people restart their businesses and provide rice to the mosques for distribution.

Thanks to people like you, we were able to deliver mammoth sacks of rice to several mosques and to help about a dozen traders re-start their businesses. Muslims who received this aid marveled that it came from American Christians when I told them the source of the good will and explained the love of Christ to them clearly – best exemplified in the cross. It was moving to play a part in this relief effort and dry people's tears, replacing dismay with hope.

I think it will be an incredible time, even when it is very hard.

Soon, I think, we will all enjoy caring for people in our communities and have the opportunity to make a bigger impact on their souls than a thousand sermons would be able to. It will be thrilling to watch all of our fellow church members get their hands dirty in ministry, a greater percentage than ever before, I believe!

Can you see how suffering refines a church? It will do the same for us. There will be no more CEO (Christmas and Easter Only) Christians in our churches when the persecution starts. All of you who are tired of the pretenders coming to Sunday services will see the meeting sizes shrink as the wheat is separated from the chaff (Matthew 13:24-30). As a side note, won't it be thrilling to see all the Scriptures that we have read for so long coming to pass? I think it will be an incredible time, even when it is very hard. I also believe God will give us abundant grace as we endure.

All of the distractions that have kept us from following hard after God will be eliminated. Daily life will consist of a focus on how everyone in our community is doing, how they can be helped that day, how the new believers can be discipled, and how God's love can be shown to the occupiers. Does that sound like Acts 4? It sure does to me. All of those sermons over the years, where pastors lamented the differences between Acts 4 and twenty-first-century churches will be made irrelevant. We will be *living* Acts 4, and no longer feeling guilty about how far we supposedly fall short, through no fault of our own, as we enjoy a fairly pain-free expression of our faith because we live in a country with freedom of religion.

What I'm trying to say is that the American Church will *never* become an Acts 4 church until the circumstances around us mirror the conditions of the early church. That day will come, my friend. And I think we will enjoy living out our faith as our predecessors did.

One source in Egypt reports the reaction of Christians to the burning of dozens of churches: "Churches are united together. And the spirit of prayer is happening in all the churches. People are praying all the time," according to a source named "David."[301]

How does that sound to you critics of the twenty-first-century church in America (this author included)? Churches united, churches praying, and people praying all the time. The church will become what we've all wanted it to become, but it may not happen until we are aggressively persecuted.

The churches in Egypt haven't stopped with simply praying. According to a *Charisma News* source in-country, Christians are answering the violence and pro-Islamic graffiti with signs that read, "You burned our church, but we love you."[302] If you were a Muslim in these cities, what would you think of such signs? I can tell you the two predominant reactions would be "Those Christians are just total weaklings" and "How does this happen? How does someone love rather than avenge?" God is certainly doing all sorts of things amid this brutal persecution, acts of salvation that we won't know about until we get to heaven.

4. Martyrdom is expected, not imagined.

How many times have you heard American Christians say, "It's not like I will ever be killed for my faith, but I have been

---

301   *http://www.charismanews.com/world/41546-many-egyptians-turning-to-christ-despite-violence-persecution* (December 20, 2013).

302   Ibid.

persecuted." Well, during the great tribulation under an Islamic Antichrist, we won't start sentences like that anymore. We will see brothers and sisters killed for their faith often, some right out of our communities. This is what is happening in the countries of the Arab Spring; martyrdom is expected, not imagined.

I have written about this in chapter 3, so I will not re-hash how and where Christians are being killed frequently in the Middle East. As so many are slaughtered simply for being Christian, we need to see how the church has reacted and the psychological impact it has had on believers. Part of a *60 Minutes* segment on the Copts featured Bob Simon exploring the tradition of martyrdom in that church. During his dramatic interview with Pope Tawadros II, Simon asked if the Copts truly believed that dying for their faith would always be a reality. The Pope replied, "In every period, we must present some martyrs. Every day, every day."[303]

Sure, we expect "suffering" as part of the Christian life, even in America, but that suffering is usually the result of a fallen world in general, not particular persecution. We see that suffering in birth defects, cancer's incursion, wayward children, and car accidents. We do not see it in people being killed for following Christ. Soon, we will know true suffering and understand so many other portions of the Bible, such as 2 Timothy 4:6-8:

> For I am already being poured out like a drink offering, and the time for my departure is near. I have fought the good fight, I have finished the race, I have kept the faith. Now there is in store for me the crown of righteousness, which the Lord, the righteous Judge, will award to me on that day – and not only to me, but also to all who have longed for his appearing.

Have you ever wondered what it would be like to utter these

---

303 *http://www.cbsnews.com/videos/the-coptic-christians-of-egypt/.*

words, knowing you are about to be killed for your faith? You might get this opportunity, and join the crowd of people who come out from under the altar as Jesus returns, those who had been martyred by the Beast (see Revelation 6:9 and 20:4), reigning on special thrones, and given authority to judge. Will we see people on those thrones whom we hear about on the evening news right now? I think we could.

5. Those usually not open to Christ will be attracted because of our testimony under fire.

Early church father Tertullian's famous line, "the blood of the martyrs is the seed of the Church," will come true before our eyes as those around us see our courage, even in the face of death, and are deeply moved. I think of a conversation I had with an incredibly committed pastor I met in Kenya during a short-term mission trip in my college years. Sitting in the back of a covered pickup truck, which acted as a bush taxi, Nathanial Kamunye had just shown me the sole of his shoe as a mutual friend urged him to. It was worn through with holes because he had walked miles to preach the gospel to unreached villages. The friend then asked Nathanial to tell me his testimony; I will never forget it, and it fits here.

Reverend Kamunye said he played an active part in the violent Mau Mau Uprising in Kenya, which sought to drive the British colonial government out by committing terrorist acts from 1952 to 1960. When Nathanial and his gang came upon a Kenyan Christian leader who they insisted was sympathetic to the British, they held a machete to his throat and ordered him to pledge his loyalty to the Mau Maus. He refused, saying that Jesus was his Lord. He did so in a very calm manner, never flinching, Nathanial said. As his throat was cut, he prayed for his killers. Nathanial never forgot that and became a Christian a short time later, entering the ministry a few years after.

Even hardened terrorists can be moved by our courage amidst suffering, and we will get our chance in America to live that out one day. General suffering will draw many to the Church, as it did after September 11, and hopefully they will stay and find Jesus. The *60 Minutes* segment showed a packed service in Cairo at a charismatic church with two thousand worshippers crammed in, and the event was broadcast nationwide. Simon asked his guide about why such services were flourishing. She replied, "There's just a sense in the community of helplessness, people in need of the priest's blessing, people in need of healing from God, people in need of support."[304]

It's sad but true; people have to feel absolutely helpless sometimes before they look to God. We will see the same phenomenon in the U.S.

Peace and courage during these sorts of times of suffering have a powerful impact on the hardest hearts. One Egyptian has reported about the church's witness there: "It's a great message of forgiveness. This makes many Muslims discover the reality of Christianity, and many of them come to know Jesus." These new believers are meeting "underground in a secret way. They worship the Lord together, and they're growing."[305]

Praise God! Only God can turn destroyed churches into a channel of salvation for many who would never consider it otherwise. He has made a long career out of bringing beauty from, in this case, literal ashes. He's doing it again in Egypt, and He will do it among us as we stand bravely for Jesus.

The final comment from the source in Egypt sums up what we can expect to see when the heat is turned up stateside. "It's always like this," he said, "when there is pressure over the

---

304 Ibid.
305 *http://www.charismanews.com/world/41546-many-egyptians-turning-to-christ-despite-violence-persecution* (December 20, 2013).

churches, the Holy Spirit is working, and many people are coming to know Jesus as Savior."[306] Indeed.

One reason why "many people are coming to know Jesus as Savior" is because once you have been directly persecuted as a Christian, any fear or shame you had about sharing your faith evaporates. Here's how one believer in the Middle East put it: "Once you experience persecution, the fear goes away … you lose it. Persecution has made me bolder in sharing my faith. That's the way persecution works. If you removed all of the verses about suffering from the Bible, there would be very little left." He added: "There is much to encourage us in God's Word. The encouragement we receive from the Lord in the Scriptures, we use to encourage each other."[307]

> *Once you have been directly persecuted as a Christian, any fear or shame you had about sharing your faith evaporates.*

So all of the seminars offered over the years on how to be bold in witnessing will be unnecessary. We will lose our fear of being identified with Christ, and we will become evangelists unlike ever before. Doesn't that sound exciting? We will see more people come to Christ as we sow more widely and without fear. And our true and genuine body life will attract many to the Savior.

How to Build a Faith That Will Withstand Any Persecution

I will close this book with a few words of hopeful wisdom to help you in case you are terrified of the future and wonder if you will be able to withstand the difficult days ahead. I do not claim in any way that I have a monopoly on how to build a solid Christian life, or some special secret to achieve rapid maturity, an oxymoron in itself. It would be impossible for you to have

306 Ibid.
307 *http://www.bibleleague.org/provide-the-bible/middle-east/muslim-man*
(December 30, 2013).

the same huge host of people build into your life that have built into mine. I'm very sorry for those of you who have had few, if any, people pour into your life by spending time with you, praying with and for you, and guiding your growth as a Christian. I have been hugely blessed in this regard.

Because of that godly input over many years and forty-plus years of walking with the Lord, I have a few ideas on how to build an unshakeable faith. People often ask me if I have doubted my faith while serving the Lord abroad in overwhelmingly Muslim communities. My answer is always "No. Being the only Christian for miles around actually builds my faith stronger." That is because I continually see the vivid contrast between the reality of Christianity and the Holy Spirit within us, and the deadness of religion, even one that calls for extremely high commitment. As I've said many times before in print and in person, ONLY the Holy Spirit can change a life, no one else. That's the primary, on-the-ground difference between Christianity and every other faith out there. The longer you are among those other faiths, even as you find elements worthy of admiration in them, you will understand that none of them actually change the heart.

So let's take a brief look at a few steps you can consider to build a faith that will remain true and strong, even if Islamists order you to forsake it.

1. Get Into a Small Group(s)

There is absolutely no need to build a strong faith through your own effort, gutting out daily Bible reading, going to church whenever you can, and trying to pray for longer and longer amounts of time each day. The modern, Western thought that we can walk with Jesus but not follow any "organized religion" is wrongheaded. This type of Lone Ranger Christianity is nowhere to be found in God's Word. It is a Western, individualistic interpretation of a faith that grew out of small groups, as we see all over the book of Acts.

I am saying clearly that you cannot grow the type of faith you will need in the End Times by watching sermons on television or online and staying in your own home with no regular contact with other Christians. The Church will never stand strong if it's built on survivalists who move as far away from others as they can and practice an isolationist Christianity.

You should not want to dive into body life simply because it is commanded. You should do it because it is enjoyable and a necessary part of your growth. We all need that sharpening from one another, as Proverbs 27:17 says, *As iron sharpens iron, so one person sharpens another.* Sociological studies that have nothing to do with the Church tell us that people are far less depressed and have a much better mental outlook when they live in social cultures. Although depression can be very hard to measure, survey after survey shows Western, wealthy countries with the highest rates.[308] I think it is due to a lack of community, not just income inequality. God made us as social beings, and we need each other to become all He wants us to be.

As I've stated before, I don't think we will have the large churches that we do now, at least not for too long. Islamists throughout history have shown a pattern of tolerating churches for a time, and then slowly, or rapidly, squeezing them to death, as we see in Arab Spring countries now. So to prepare for that type of approach in America, we are going to have to perfect the fine art of being a good small group member and/or leader. To practice that, get into at least one small group and experience the joy of mutual encouragement in Christ. I would urge you to join one of the small groups offered at your church; if

---

308 *http://www.cnn.com/2011/HEALTH/07/26/affluent.depression.prone/*
(January 9, 2013), one example of a major study showing poor countries less depressed than rich ones.

there are none, start one. You will begin to build the kind of community life that will be needed when crisis hits.

In addition to that weekly small group, consider starting an even smaller group by either discipling someone who is not as far along in the faith as you are, or being discipled by someone who has spent more time walking closely with God. If those words make you uncomfortable or you do not know anyone on a different spiritual level than you, find an accountability partner to meet with and be transparent with as you talk and pray together.

I would argue for some sort of discipleship relationship if at all possible. There is nothing more powerful than spending time with someone who is further along in the faith than you are. This is a very biblical model (see 2 Timothy 2:2) that we somehow neglect once we get out of the parachurch ministries we were in during our college years. Why?

Find a saint in your church who is further along than you, someone you click with and respect deeply, and ask him or her to spend time with you over the next several months. People shy away from long-term commitments, and many cannot keep them due to changing schedules and high mobility, but begin with a weekly or bi-weekly meeting to start. Tell your prospective discipler you want to go through a certain book of the Bible or another Christian book that you both like.[309] Then, set a regular time to meet, pray together, confess your sins to each other, and keep in constant touch. I would also recommend doing some sort of ministry together, whether that be volunteering in the children's ministry, participating on the worship team, helping at a soup kitchen, or chaperoning a youth retreat. Don't just make your relationship an intellectual one; form a true bond and include kingdom building in it.

---

309 See *http://www.coregroups.org/* as an example of the type of resources available, often for free.

If you are already fairly far along in your faith, find someone who is newer in the faith and you fill the role of discipler. You will learn at least as much in the role of big brother or sister. Find a person not as mature as you and challenge him or her to meet with you regularly to go deeper with God. You will *never* regret taking this risk on either side of the discipleship relationship. This will also give you someone to cling to when the

You will no longer be able to outsource your kids' spiritual development.

going gets tough, in addition to your best friends, spouse, and other family members, and it will help to build you into a mature follower of Christ. When Jesus wanted to start a movement, He didn't only preach to large crowds. He selected twelve men to pour His life into, a common model of apprenticeship back then, and one I've seen in developing countries even today.

It's not possible for us to quit our jobs and simply walk around and pour biblical wisdom into people. However, the effectiveness and relevance of this method remain true. We need to follow the example of Christ in our down time and spend at least part of those hours being a disciple and discipling others. When we are discussing the deep truths of Scripture and life with another person, we can learn so much from someone else's perspective, whether that be someone who has seen a lot more of life than we have, or someone who is fairly new to the Christian life and has a child-like faith and excitement. In this case, two or three heads is way, way better than one.

Get into a small group if you haven't already, and get into a two- or three-person discipleship group as well, to build a rock-solid faith.

Of course, this sort of discipleship must begin in the home. During the Great Tribulation, you will no longer be able to outsource your kids' spiritual development. Mom, Dad, you are going to have to pass on the faith as never before, and model what it means to follow Jesus at all costs. I'm not saying that you should pull your children out of AWANA or Young Life. I am saying that if you have NO spiritual input into your kids' lives, if you never pray with them, never open the Word with them, and never talk about spiritual matters with them, you need to change. Call a once-a-week family devotion time for starters, and have a small group meeting around the dinner table some nights. Ask your kids how you can pray for them and enjoy the sweet sound of hearing them pray as well. They will teach you a lot about following the Lord, believe me, as the faith is expressed in the coming generation.

When all is said and done, the most basic unit of faith will be your family. What kind of spiritual dynamic is there now in your family? Any at all? It's time to alter your family culture a bit, perhaps, to include discussion, prayer, and study of what it means to live all out for God. Take small steps and begin to re-take direction of your children's spiritual development.

2. Get Into the Word

This point is fairly obvious, I would hope. Don't view it as a burden or a homework assignment. I'm not going to tell you to read through the Bible in a year, although that is great. But aim for consistency, even if in small portions. Remember that the Word should be a joy, a light unto your path, a stress-reliever, a solace, something that lightens your spirit. If you are totally bored with your devotions, change them up.

- Find a different version of the Bible to make the Word sound new and fresh.

- Listen to the Bible on your phone or on a CD while driving.

- Meditate on just a phrase or verse per day.

- Read books and commentaries on a given book that you like and unlock the deeper meanings of it.

The reason we need a constant, consistent exposure to the Word is because the world is trying to brainwash us with a very different system of thought. It is relentless, through daily conversations, advertisements, television programs and movies, music, and on and on. Some of what we see on TV is great, and some movies are masterpieces. But the world in general is against God and either subtly, or overtly, wants to weaken your faith. And it will, given enough time, unless you counterbalance it with the eternal truth of Scripture.

As 1 John 2:15-16 reminds us:

> *Do not love the world or anything in the world. If anyone loves the world, the love of the Father is not in them. For everything in the world – the lust of the flesh, the lust of the eyes, and the pride of life – comes not from the Father but from the world.*

Let me restate the paragraph above: You WILL have a much weaker faith if you do not chew on God's Word on a consistent basis. That is a guarantee. There is too much other stuff in the world that will cause you to doubt and compromise.

Get into the Bible every day if you can – make it fun and novel. I read Scripture in different languages to give it a new twist, and I also like to hear it orally from time to time. I also have the blessing of writing devotions as a part of making a living as a writer/editor, and that allows me to ruminate on Scripture every week. I try to always have a book on my bedside table by a writer that I respect on some biblical book or theme. These authors open up Scripture to me in a way I never could do on my own. At the time of this writing, I'm re-reading *King's Cross* by Timothy Keller and have just begun *Encounters with Jesus* by Keller as well. Both are provoking a lot of deep thought and providing me with brand-new insights into Scripture.

What can you do to keep your Bible reading fresh? Brainstorm for a while and write down a few ideas. Keep your intake of the Bible regular and enjoyable. May it never seem like an obligation!

One particular theme you might want to drill down on is what the Holy Spirit said to men and women who were undergoing tremendous suffering for their faith. Peter's first letter is of great help here, as is the entire book of Hebrews. Almost all of Paul's letters have at least one section designed to encourage his readers to abide in Christ and not deny the Lord. Ephesians 6 is a great example of this. The New Testament verses on the topic of persecution will have particular resonance as you are ordered to adopt Islam as your faith or face a severe penalty.

3. Pray Without Ceasing

This is a commandment from the Lord (see 1 Thessalonians 5:17) that should seem like anything *but* a yoke to you. It's actually a great way to live.

I don't want to sound like a super-spiritual person with all of the answers, but I honestly can't make it through the day without talking to God continually. I need Him to calm me at times, to come through for me at times, to enable me to forgive others at times, to inspire me at times, and to give me the right words at times. I really need Him – and you do too!

People around you might think you're crazy as you pray without ceasing, especially if you do it verbally, even in hushed tones. I don't recommend walking down the street and proclaiming your prayers in a loud voice. That will drive more people *away* from God than *to* Jesus, but if you do need to say your prayers out loud, as I do, either do it quietly or get to a place where you can be a little louder. Frankly, an hour of silent prayer will put me to sleep. I do not have the discipline of a monk.

So, what I do is get alone a few times a day and talk out loud with God, pouring out my concerns and staying quiet for certain periods to hear His replies. It's a lot of fun talking to

God all day, throughout my day. I think it is the type of relationship He wants to have with us, and I think it will be the kind of closeness we will need when times get trying. Start this practice now and build an ongoing walk with God that will give you a continual sense of His presence. Nothing is so mundane that the Lord doesn't care about it.

Nothing is so mundane that the Lord doesn't care about it.

A book that I really appreciate on this topic is called *The Reflective Life* by Ken Gire. His thesis is that nothing in the course of a day is by chance. We should try to understand what God is trying to communicate to us, all during the day, in every conversation, every emotion, and every incident taking place right in front of us. This is a book that I would highly recommend to you as you practice the presence of God each day and pray without ceasing.

4. Get Involved in Ministry

Many times when you share your faith and the love of Jesus, your faith becomes much more real to you. The old saying that "involvement breeds commitment" is also true. If you want to increase your commitment to Christ, jump into a ministry and watch how God comes through in many cool ways. You will also discover that every time you share your faith, it is reinforced in your mind as being true, kind of like how writing something down helps you to remember it.

I have found this true again and again in my own life. When I stop sharing my faith, or even a bit of it in a conversation with someone, it can grow cold and stale, just part of my head knowledge and sterile philosophy of life, not something in my heart that excites and inspires me. However, when I take the opportunities that God gives me and share a bit of the Good News with someone, I remember again just how true and trustworthy my faith in Jesus is. This is a spiritual truth that you can bank on. As I run into people who are receptive to the gospel, I am reminded again of how powerful and life-changing it can be. Each time we watch Jesus change a person, we are reminded that He is alive and working today, that He is indeed *the way and the truth and the life* (see John 14:6). If we never share our faith, we will lose out on this continual re-demonstration of the power of the Spirit. When was the last time you were around a new Christian? Was their excitement about their new life in Jesus infectious? Of course it was. If you want to be around those types of people, then you need to share the gospel!

Another advantage of getting involved in ministry is you can become publicly identified with a cause, and perhaps take a bit of grief for it, which will only reinforce your commitment to the kingdom. Douglas Hyde describes this in detail in his classic work *Dedication and Leadership*,[310] where he makes the point that the Communist Party in Great Britain always put new recruits in the public eye right away so they would be forever cemented to the movement. We don't do that enough in the Church! Serve as part of a literature distribution team and hear someone make a nasty comment to you. Give your time at a church car wash and have a visitor tell you, "I don't believe any of this B.S." The conversation you have will serve to deepen your faith. Man a table at a community fair for your church and hear someone attack the church for its many weaknesses. Anything you can do to experience a low level of persecution will get you more ready for larger and more serious forms of persecution.

Diving into ministry also gives Jesus an opportunity to fulfill all of the promises He has made to you and me. If we stay in our personal comfort zones all of the time and never take a risk for God – leading a small group, helping with youth

---

310 Douglas Hyde, *Dedication and Leadership* (South Bend, IN: University of Notre Dame Press, 1992).

ministry, planning an outreach – then we never see Him come through in a mighty way, and words like "I will never leave you nor forsake you," "I will give you the words to say," and "You will receive power and you will be my witnesses" become dusty statements that sit on the pages of your Bible, not a life reality. You will experience a jolt of joy and adrenaline as you return home from a great small group that you just led, from a discipleship appointment that proved you were helping someone, from an evangelistic event that attracted dozens from the community. You will never know that jolt and joy until you go out on a limb for God.

I don't have the time or page space to share extensively with you how true this has been in my own life. When I look back on the chances I've taken for God and how He has come through, I am astounded and grateful, and it makes me want to take more chances for Him. Two huge challenges spring to mind – taking a family of four into a dirt-poor African neighborhood to start a church among Muslims, and selling everything I have to go to a country that is 99 percent Islamic to find seekers and share my faith. I had a sanctified insanity in both cases, and God opened doors both times that no man could shut. He is good. He is there. He wants to show you His power and love, but you're going to have to get off the couch to bond with Him as you work together.

To put this in more human terms, think of the best ways that you can grow close to someone. It's one thing to share a cup of coffee with someone. It's another to clean a house or paint a room or construct a play set with him or her. Working with someone physically produces a special bond, doesn't it? *It's the same with God.* As you say "Yes" to His promptings and get into a ministry, you will discover a special bond with Him as well. "Thanks, God, I never knew I could do that" will be a common statement, and this closeness will prove vital when someone urges you to deny your faith.

5. Meditate on God as Loving Father

Of all the scriptural truths that we will need to grip tightly as we go through hard times, this might be the most important of them all. I would encourage you to spend a lot of time on this biblical concept, making certain verses and chapters the places you go back to again and again to meditate on. Say to yourself as you look at these passages, "God loves me like a wonderful Daddy." He really does, and we don't talk enough about it. Some of us had poor role models as dads; others of us had abusive dads, absentee dads, or dads who didn't show physical affection, etc. For that reason, we have an incorrect concept of our heavenly Father. That's a shame, and it hurts us more than you might realize. When we get into a tight fix, we don't trust God because we couldn't trust our father. When life throws difficult circumstances our way, we are sure God is against us, because we never had a father who was for us. Our view of God colors our entire outlook on life. As best-selling author and prophet A. W. Tozer said, "What comes into our minds when we think about God is the most important thing about us."[311]

In my case, my alcoholic father was fairly absentee. We saw each other every other weekend from the time I was ten onward. Even when I lived with my dad or stayed with him for a weekend, he was kind of half there, often intoxicated, and a little fuzzy. So, what do I think about God when I come face to face with a hard circumstance? I conclude, "He's fuzzy. He's not around. He's busy somewhere else. He doesn't care." This is a knee-jerk reaction that I have battled for decades, and most of you know exactly what I am talking about. We need to

311 http://www.goodreads.com/quotes/376518-what-comes-into-our-minds-when-we-think-about-god (January 2, 2014).

replace these thoughts of correlation with biblical truth, which tells us that God is NEVER fuzzy, ALWAYS present, ABIDING forever inside us.

If we think of God as a super-loving Dad, then we will realize that no matter how much we suffer, it is temporal, and He is indeed preparing a better, eternal place for us. I think of times I've asked my children to go through a difficult trial, many times unintentionally and due to my own stupidity, but I watched as their knowledge of my love helped them to persevere.

God is NEVER fuzzy, ALWAYS present, ABIDING forever inside us.

One day in southern France during a summer when I served as an interim pastor, I wanted to introduce my family to the wonders of whitewater rafting. It's a great sport, but in France it is often not at all regulated. We did a bit of research and found what looked like a fairly peaceful river and a place to rent canoes in a lovely part of a gorgeous country.

It was a beautiful day, about 70 degrees, and sunny. The water was running fairly swiftly but didn't look like trouble. How little we knew! The gentleman who rented out the canoes said little about the river's perils, probably assuming that we were canoeing vets. He did urge us to put all of our extra clothes and items into a waterproof plastic container that came with the canoes. We wondered why he was recommending this so strongly, given the seemingly tranquil waters.

We got about halfway down the river and then experienced several areas of whitewater rapids, narrow passageways, turbulent water, and general mayhem. My wife and daughter capsized at least twice, while my son and I flipped once, with me screaming at him profanely over his need to paddle while I pushed when we got stuck. It was not my finest moment.

As socks, shoes, shirts, and other items of clothing drifted down the river, my son and I pulled to shore first, where a bus was scheduled to pick up all canoeists and kayakers. I went back into the water to retrieve most of my daughter's items, which had floated downstream. A couple of French people graciously waded out into the water to help me, stunned at the wreckage and the obvious shock my daughter was in as the trip concluded. They mumbled about the idiocy of inexperienced canoeists taking on such a wild river. It was a memorable day, to say the least.

I apologized profusely to my family for my conduct and my bad idea; they forgave me quickly. I would like to think that my children knew – just knew – that their father would see them through that very trying day. I looked my children right in the eye as I told them to stay calm at certain times and urged them to continue on. They did because they trusted me. In my case, they probably shouldn't have, but we can *always* trust God, even in whitewater. Nothing can separate us from His love (see Romans 8:38-39), and He has compassion on us as a father has compassion on his children (see Psalm 103:13-14). I hugged all of my kids tightly after our ill-advised river escapade, and God wants to hug us all amidst the difficulties in our own lives.

Spend a lot of time thinking about God as your loving Father, and hang on to that biblical truth as your circumstances change.

6. Do Some Study in Apologetics
This bit of counsel might not apply to some of you, but it really helped me to establish a granite foundation for my faith. During my college years, I asked myself if I believed Christianity just because I was immersed in the Church from age ten to seventeen, or because I *knew* it was true. I experienced several challenges to my faith in college, particularly from professors who belittled my beliefs and forcefully taught worldviews contrary to biblical Christianity, such as evolution and circumstantial

morality based on the lack of any one, permanent truth for all times and all peoples.

At the time I was in college, Josh McDowell was the number-one apologist for our faith, and I devoured his books. I read them carefully to satisfy my desire to know that Christianity was solid intellectually and not just a religious culture that I happened to emerge from. Those years of study have been important to me in maintaining my faith ever since, even thirty years later. I go back to the historical, not shaky, truths of Christ's resurrection, the miracle of the Bible's transmission, secular historians' accounts of the life of Jesus, and many other points to remember that my faith is absolutely true and worth holding onto. I remember the strong arguments for the historicity of Christ's resurrection, from which our entire faith flows (see 1 Corinthians 15). It truly did happen, and no serious historian will question that. Paul made this connection between the sureness of the resurrection and holding onto our faith as persecution rages when he wrapped up 1 Corinthians 15: *Therefore* [in light of all I've said about the resurrection in this chapter], *my dear brothers and sisters, stand firm. Let nothing move you. Always give yourselves fully to the work of the Lord, because you know that your labor in the Lord is not in vain* (v. 58).

I know all about how this modern age is one of image, not text, of love, not reason, etc., and I'm told that no one even cares if Christianity is true anymore, only that it is a good story. Even so, if you have never taken the time to bolster your faith in your head and mind, read a few books that will fortify you for the days to come. I would recommend everything from McDowell's books and *Mere Christianity* by C. S. Lewis, to books by Timothy Keller, Ravi Zacharias, Os Guinness, Lee Strobel, and Norman Geisler. Any of these authors can add an intellectual bulwark in your mind and spirit that will help you to stay strong.

Conclusion

You have probably heard all of the advice in the preceding thirty pages or so already. I hope I have prompted at least one new thought for you to strengthen your Christian life, but I am aware that thousands of books have been written on how to grow in Christ. Many of you are already doing what I wrote about in the previous chapter. You will be leaders when your town is visited by the religious police, as they go door to door to find out how much Christian resistance is in the burg.

For those of you who are leading an apathetic Christian life that consists of little more than attending worship and dropping off the kids for children's programs, I would encourage you, in love, to grab hold of the adventure that God wants to give you as you walk hand in hand with Him. God does NOT want you to be bored with Him. He does want to push you further than you ever thought you could go, in knowledge of Scripture, in ministry involvement, in building into others' lives, and in leading your family.

The point of the previous chapter is to clearly communicate that being a pew-sitter will not enable you to stand firm until the end. It would hurt me to think that any person who read my first book, or this one, would be among those who fall away when the pressure comes. Scripture talks about this class of people much more than we want to admit. Here's one sample passage, straight from the mouth of Christ:

Then you will be handed over to be persecuted and put
to death, and you will be hated by all nations because
of me. At that time many will turn away from the faith
and will betray and hate each other, and many false
prophets will appear and deceive many people. Because
of the increase of wickedness, the love of most will grow
cold, but the one who stands firm to the end will be
saved. (Matthew 24:9-13)

I think of two images as I read these words. One is from the
movie *The War of the Worlds* starring Tom Cruise. I thought
that film did an outstanding job of depicting how people do not
have the tendency to look out for others when terrible danger
surrounds them. Rather, it is usually every man for himself.
I'll never forget the scene where Cruise and his children try to
board one of the ships pulling out of the harbor as the ramp
pulls up and people scramble to hold on by their fingertips,
some dropping into the sea. This is the atmosphere that we
will be in when high-pressure persecution begins, when we
are handed over to death and are hated.

Another image I recall was the face of a French person with
whom I discussed that country's history. I asked why French
people were so private, so skeptical, and not trusting of their
fellow man. My friend replied that French people have betrayed
each other many times in their history. The first time was when
Catholics killed Protestants (resulting in a half-Protestant
country becoming only 2 percent Protestant in population), and
then during World War II, when the French again turned in
Vichy supporters who were planning acts of terrorism against
the occupying Nazis.

When our occupiers come in, many will be tempted to
switch to their side and betray their neighbors – even their

families. No doubt, it will be easy to turn away from the faith, to hate and betray.

I've written this short book to prepare us all for a time when this temptation will be great, in the hopes that no one who turns these pages will fall away. Let us all stand firm to the end and be saved! May none of us have a love that grows cold, as some run and others sell us out. May we all have a depth of faith that will never be swayed, refusing to repeat any other confession of faith than that in Christ Jesus. Remember, they can kill the body, but they can't kill the spirit.

Jesus told us to not despair over the horrible period before His return. His words in Luke 21:28 should be among the last words of this book: *When these things begin to take place, stand up and lift up your heads, because your redemption is drawing near.*

I trust that this book has helped you to "stand up" in the sense of this verse. The choice to raise your head is yours.

About the Author

Ralph Stice has lived in Islamic communities on three continents over 11 years' time as a witness for Christ. During that time, he has interacted with a wide variety of Muslims at many levels of society. He also has read widely on the subject of Islam and has spoken in nearly 100 churches about the world's second-largest religion. He has recently founded RWS Ministries, a non-profit organization determined to inform Christians about Islam and inform Muslims about Jesus's true identity and lordship. He blogs frequently on developments in the Islamic world and is a keen observer of political and spiritual developments in the Middle East.

Connect with Ralph

 www.rwsministries.com

www.facebook.com/524183586

Throughout the long history of the church, men have searched in vain to discover the ideal model for the corporate structure of the church. No hierarchy is clearly spelled out in the Scriptures except what the Spirit says through Paul in the letter to the Corinthians or the Ephesians. Nevertheless, throughout the age of the church, many individuals and groups involved in wars and with blood on their hands have not hesitated to attempt to build the temple of the Lord in the form of a given denomination, group, or organized movement. These attempts resulted in building dead monuments instead of joining living stones that would be a light unto the nations. Man measures success according to the criteria of this world, the number of participants, or some other outward measurement, while God measures success by righteousness in the heart and obedience to His Word by those who have learned His ways.

What About the Church
Russell Stendal
ISBN: 978-1-62245-092-3

Most Christians know that all is not well with America. Every day we feel pushed further to the margins of society. We are losing status, influence, and certain freedoms. What is the church to do?

In *Return to the Margins* Terry Coy explains that the church has historically and globally existed and thrived at the margins. Jesus ministered in the margins of society. The New Testament church grew from the margins. Most of the global church today lives and ministers in the margins. The church in post-Christian America must understand:

- What the new norm will look like for the American church
- What to do when religious rights are taken away
- What the church must do now to prepare for a return to the margins
- How life in the margins has historically increased the church's fruitfulness

Return to the Margins
Terry Coy
ISBN: 978-1-62245-229-3

The book of Revelation is a love letter to the church. Yet most view it as troubling, and many misunderstand what the Lord is trying to tell us. Didn't the Jews in Jesus' day have some of the same problems?

Early biblical prophecy, already fulfilled, helps define what is about to happen. Are some bad, scary events looming on the horizon? Yes, and you'll learn about that. But even more important, you'll see what Scripture has to say about you as the overcomer. The puzzles of Revelation are coming together, and we who love and serve the Lord are seeing that the best is yet to come.

Revelation: The Best is Yet to Come
Jim Richards
ISBN: 978-1-62245-180-7

The Bible contains much prophecy concerning end times, warning us to not be ignorant so we can be bold and fight the good fight of faith. As Christians, we'll predictably face more hostility and possibly increased persecution in America as we draw closer to Jesus Christ's return. It is now more pivotal than ever that we prepare ourselves, know the truth of Scripture, and understand the direction our country has taken.

ERADICATE: Blotting Out God in America
David Fiorazo
ISBN: 978-1-62245-026-8

jubilee
B I B L E   2000

Hear what God is
saying through this
original translation

ANEKO Press